BECOMING A WARRIOR
FOR AN ENLIGHTENED HUMANITY

Over the past seven years, I have been presenting a series of "Shambhala teachings" that use the image of the Shambhala kingdom to represent the ideal of secular enlightenment. The Shambhala teachings are founded on the premise that there *is* basic human wisdom that can help to solve the world's problems. This wisdom does not belong to any one culture or religion, nor does it come only from the West or the East. Rather, it is a tradition of human warriorship that has existed in many cultures at many times throughout history. Warriorship in this context is the tradition of human bravery, or the tradition of fearlessness. The key to warriorship and the first principle of Shambhala vision is not being afraid of who you are.

If we want to help the world, we have to make a personal journey. It is up to each of us individually to find the meaning of enlightened society and how it can be realized. It is my hope that this presentation of the path of the Shambhala warrior may contribute to the dawning of this discovery.

BANTAM NEW AGE BOOKS

This important imprint includes books in a variety of fields and disciplines and deals with the search for meaning, growth and change. They are books that circumscribe our times and our future.

Ask your bookseller for the books you have missed.

SHAMBHALA

THE SACRED PATH OF THE WARRIOR

 CHÖGYAM TRUNGPA

Edited by Carolyn Rose Gimian

BANTAM BOOKS
TORONTO · NEW YORK · LONDON · SYDNEY · AUCKLAND

SHAMBHALA: THE SACRED PATH OF THE WARRIOR
*A Bantam Book / published by arrangement with
Shambhala Publications, Inc.*

PRINTING HISTORY
Shambhala edition published April 1984
4 printings through March 1986
*Serialized in Yoga Journal, November/December 1984; and
Inside Kung-Fu, March 1985.*
Bantam edition / October 1986

*The material that appears on pages xi, 3, 65, 123, and 155 is
from a text of Shambhala. The excerpts from the text and their
translation are included in the copyrights of this book.*
*On page xviii, Mr. James George is quoted from his article
"Searching for Shambhala," from Search, edited by Jean Sulzberger,
copyright © by Jean Sulzberger. Reprinted by permission of Harper
and Row, Publishers Inc.*

*New Age and the accompanying figure design as well as the statement
"a search for meaning, growth, and change" are trademarks of
Bantam Books, Inc.*

Line drawings on the front cover by Sherap Palden Beru.

ISBN 0-553-26172-X

Published simultaneously in the United States and Canada

*Bantam Books are published by Bantam Books, Inc. Its trade-
mark, consisting of the words "Bantam Books" and the por-
trayal of a rooster, is Registered in U.S. Patent and Trademark
Office and in other countries. Marca Registrada. Bantam
Books, Inc., 666 Fifth Avenue, New York, New York 10103.*

PRINTED IN THE UNITED STATES OF AMERICA

O   0 9 8 7 6 5 4 3 2 1

TO GESAR OF LING

༄༅། །ཐེག་པ་ཐ་མའི་དམིགས་ཤིང་།
ལུག་སེ་པ་བྱུང་འཁྲུག་དཔལ་དང་ལྷུག
བཙོ་ལས་འདས་པའི་ཀྲེ་བཙེད་ཅམ།
རིགས་ལྔན་རྒྱལ་པོའི་ཞབས་ལ་འདུད།།

He who has neither beginning nor end
Who possesses the glory of Tiger Lion Garuda Dragon
Who possesses the confidence beyond words
I pay homage at the feet of the Rigden King

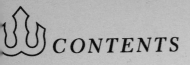
CONTENTS

ILLUSTRATIONS

Front cover. Animals representing the four dignities (see Chapter Twenty) in the heart center of a garuda, which is emerging from a sun disc. The translation of the Tibetan inscription is: "Profound, Brilliant, Just, Powerful, All-Victorious." *Design by Chögyam Trungpa.*

Inside front and back pages. Line drawings of the tiger, lion, garuda, and dragon *by Sherap Palden Beru.*

p. 34. Design by Chögyam Trungpa. Executed by Gina Janowitz.

p. 53. The blazing three jewels, representing the principles of richness and command. *Design by Chögyam Trungpa. Executed by Molly Nudell.*

p. 103. The Chinese character for the emperor. The bottom half is the character for the ruler or king described on page 102. *Calligraphy by Sheng-Piao Kiang. Photography by George Holmes.*

p. 130. Wangthang, or "authentic presence." *Calligraphy by Chögyam Trungpa. Photograph by George Holmes.*

p. 134. Design by Chögyam Trungpa. Executed by Molly Nudell.

〇 *EDITOR'S PREFACE*

CHÖGYAM TRUNGPA is best known to Western readers as the author of several popular books on the Buddhist teachings, including *Cutting Through Spiritual Materialism, The Myth of Freedom,* and *Meditation in Action.* The present volume, *Shambhala,* is a major departure from these earlier works. Although the author acknowledges the relationship of the Shambhala teachings to Buddhist principles and although he discusses at some length the practice of sitting meditation—which is virtually identical to Buddhist meditation practice—nevertheless, this book presents an unmistakably secular rather than religious outlook. There are barely a half-dozen foreign terms used in the manuscript, and in tone and content this volume speaks directly—sometimes painfully so—to the experience and the challenge of being human.

Even in the name with which he signs the Foreword—Dorje Dradul of Mukpo—the author distinguishes this book from his other works. *Shambhala* is about the path of warriorship, or the path of bravery, that is open to any human being who seeks a genuine and fearless existence. The title *Dorje Dradul* means the "indestructible" or "adamantine warrior." Mukpo is the author's family name, which was replaced at an early age by his Buddhist title, Chögyam Trungpa, Rinpoche. In Chapter Eleven, "Nowness," the author describes the importance that the name Mukpo holds for him and gives us some hints of why he chooses to use it in the context of this book.

Although the author uses the legend and imagery of the Shambhala kingdom as the basis for his presentation, he states quite clearly that he is not presenting the Buddhist *Kalacakra* teachings on Shambhala. Instead, this volume draws on ancient, perhaps even primordial, wisdom and principles of human conduct, as manifested in the traditional, pre-industrial societies of Tibet, India, China, Japan, and Korea. In particular, this book draws its imagery and inspiration from the warrior culture of Tibet, which predated Buddhism and remained a basic influence on Tibetan society until the Communist Chinese invasion in 1959. Yet, whatever its sources, the vision that is presented here has not been articulated anywhere else. It is a unique statement on the human condition and potential, which is made more remarkable by its haunting and familiar ring—it is as though we had always known the truths contained here.

The author's interest in the kingdom of Shambhala dates back to his years in Tibet, where he was the supreme abbot of the Surmang monasteries. As a young man, he studied some of the tantric texts that discuss the legendary kingdom of Shambhala, the path to it, and its inner significance. As he was fleeing from the Communist Chinese over the Himalayas in 1959, Chögyam Trungpa was writing a spiritual account of the history of Shambhala, which unfortunately was lost on the journey. Mr. James George, former Canadian High Commissioner to India and a personal friend of the author, reports that in 1968 Chögyam Trungpa told him that "although he had never been there [Shambhala], he believed in its existence and could see it in his mirror whenever he went into deep meditation." Mr. George then tells us how he later witnessed the author gazing into a small handmirror and describing in detail the kingdom of Shambhala. As Mr. George says: ". . . There was Trungpa in our study describing what he saw as if he were looking out of the window."

In spite of this longstanding interest in the kingdom of Shambhala, when Chögyam Trungpa first came to the West, he seems to have refrained from any mention of Shambhala, other than passing references. It was only in 1976, a few months before beginning a year's retreat, that he began to emphasize the importance of the Shambhala teachings. At the 1976 Vajradhatu Seminary, an advanced three-month training course for two hundred students, Chögyam Trungpa gave several talks on the Shambhala principles. Then, during his 1977 retreat, the author began a series of writings on Shambhala, and he requested his students to initiate a secular, public program of meditation, to which he gave the name "Shambhala Training."

Since that time, the author has given well over a hundred lectures on themes connected with Shambhala vision. Some of these talks have been given to students in the Shambhala Training program, many of them have been addressed to the directors, or teachers, of Shambhala Training, a few of the lectures were given as public talks in major cities in the United States, and one group of talks constituted a public seminar entitled "The Warrior of Shambhala," taught jointly with Ösel Tendzin at Naropa Institute in Boulder, Colorado in the summer of 1979.

To prepare this volume, the editors, under the author's guidance, reviewed all of the lectures on the subject matter and searched for the best, or most appropriate, treatments of particular topics. In addition, the author wrote original material for this book, notably the discussion of the dignities of meek, perky, and outrageous that appears in Chapter Twenty, "Authentic Presence." He had already composed the material on inscrutability as an essay during his 1977 retreat, and the discussion of the other three dignities was written for this book in a style compatible with the original article.

In deciding upon the sequence of chapters and the logical progression of the topics, the original lectures were themselves the foremost guide. In studying this material the editors found that the Shambhala teachings present, not only the logic of the mind, but also the logic of the heart. Based as much on intuition as on intellect, these teachings weave a complex and sometimes crisscrossing picture of human experience. To preserve this character, the editors chose to draw the structure of the book out of the structure of the original lectures themselves. Of necessity, this sometimes resulted in paradoxical or even seemingly contradictory treatments of a topic. Yet we found that the overall elegance and integrity of the material were best served by retaining the inherent logic of the original presentation, with all its complexities.

Respect for the integrity of the original lectures was also the guiding principle in the treatment of language. In his presentation of the Shambhala principles, the author takes common words in the English language, such as "goodness," and gives them uncommon, often extraordinary, meanings. By doing so, Chögyam Trungpa elevates everyday experience to the level of sacredness, and at the same time, he brings esoteric concepts, such as magic, into the realm of ordinary understanding and perception. This is often done by stretching the English language to accommodate subtle understanding within seeming simplicity. In our editing, we tried to retain and bring out the author's voice rather than suppress it, feeling that this approach would best convey the power of the material.

Before work on *Shambhala* began, many of the author's talks had already been edited for use by students and teachers in the Shambhala Training program. These early editorial efforts by Mr. Michael Kohn, Mrs. Judith Lief, Mrs. Sarah Levy, Mr. David Rome, Mrs. Barbara Blouin, and Mr. Frank Berliner are gratefully acknowledged; they considerably reduced the task of preparing this book.

The curriculum used in Shambhala Training was of great help in organizing the material for this book, and thanks are due to those who have worked with the author to develop and revise this curriculum over the past six years: Mr. David Rome, private secretary to the author and the assistant to the publisher at Schocken Books; Dr. Jeremy Hayward, vice president of the Nalanda Foundation; Mrs. Lila Rich, executive director of Shambhala Training; as well as the staff of Shambhala Training, notably Mr. Frank Berliner, Mrs. Christie Baker, and Mr. Dan Holmes.

Ongoing guidance was provided by Ösel Tendzin, the cofounder of Shambhala Training and Chögyam Trungpa's dharma heir, who reviewed the original proposal for the book and gave critical feedback on the manuscript at various stages of completion. We are extremely grateful for his participation in this project.

A similar role was played by Mr. Samuel Bercholz, the publisher of Shambhala Publications. As shown by the name he gave to his company in 1968, Mr. Bercholz has a deeply rooted connection to Shambhala and its wisdom. His belief in this project and his constant interest in it were a major force in moving the manuscript along and bringing it to completion.

Two of the editors at Vajradhatu deserve special mention for their excellent work on the manuscript: Mrs. Sarah Levy and Mrs. Donna Holm. In addition, we would like to offer particular thanks to Mr. Ken Wilber, the editor of the New Science Library and the author of *Up from Eden* and other books. Mr. Wilber read the manuscript in both penultimate and final form, and his detailed and pointed comments led to significant changes in the final text.

Mr. Robert Walker served as the administrative assistant to the editors, and without the secretarial and support services that he provided, this book never could have been completed. His excellent and diligent contribution to the project deserves our greatest thanks. Mrs. Rachel Anderson also served as an administrative assistant for a period of several months, and we thank her for her dedicated help. It is not possible to mention by name the many volunteers who produced the transcriptions that already existed when we began work on the book, but their efforts are gratefully acknowledged.

The editors also wish to thank the Nalanda Translation Group for the translations from the Tibetan that appear here, in particular Mr. Ugyen Shenpen, who calligraphed the original Tibetan writings. We also thank the editorial and production staff at Shambhala Publications for their assistance, notably Mr. Larry Mermelstein, Miss Emily Hilburn, and Mrs. Hazel Bercholz.

We thank as well the many other readers who took time to review and comment on the final manuscript: Mr. Marvin

Casper, Mr. Michael Chender, Lodrö Dorje, Dr. Larry Dossey, Dr. Wendy Goble, Dr. James Green, Miss Lynn Hildebrand, Miss Lynn Milot, Ms. Susan Purdy, Mr. Eric Skjei, Mrs. Susan Niemack Skjei, Mr. Joseph Spieler, Mr. Jeff Stone, and Mr. Joshua Zim. We particularly thank Dr. Goble for her careful copyediting of the final text.

It is impossible to express adequate thanks to the author—both for his vision in presenting the Shambhala teachings and for the privilege of assisting him with the editing of this book. In addition to working closely with the editors on the manuscript, he seemed able to provide an atmosphere of magic and power that pervaded and inspired this project. This is a somewhat outrageous thing to say, but once having read this book, perhaps the reader will find it not so strange a statement. It felt as though the author empowered this text so that it could rise above the poor vision of its editors and proclaim its wisdom. We hope only that we have not obstructed or weakened the power of these teachings. May they help to liberate all beings from the warring evils of the setting sun.

CAROLYN ROSE GIMIAN

Boulder, Colorado
October 1983

⟨⟩ FOREWORD

I AM SO DELIGHTED to be able to present the vision of Shambhala in this book. It is what the world needs and what the world is starved for. I would like to make it clear, however, that this book does not reveal any of the secrets from the Buddhist tantric tradition of Shambhala teachings, nor does it present the philosophy of the *Kalacakra*. Rather, this book is a manual for people who have lost the principles of sacredness, dignity, and warriorship in their lives. It is based particularly on the principles of warriorship as they were embodied in the ancient civilizations of India, Tibet, China, Japan, and Korea. This book shows how to refine one's way of life and how to propagate the true meaning of warriorship. It is inspired by the example and the wisdom of the great Tibetan king, Gesar of Ling—his inscrutability and fearlessness and the way in which he conquered barbarianism by using the principles of Tiger, Lion, Garuda, Dragon (Tak, Seng, Khyung, Druk), which are discussed in this book as the four dignities.

I am honored and grateful that in the past I have been

able to present the wisdom and dignity of human life within the context of the religious teachings of Buddhism. Now it gives me tremendous joy to present the principles of Shambhala warriorship and to show how we can conduct our lives as warriors with fearlessness and rejoicing, without destroying one another. In this way, the vision of the Great Eastern Sun (Sharchen Nyima) can be promoted, and the goodness in everyone's heart can be realized without doubt.

DORJE DRADUL OF MUKPO

Boulder, Colorado
August 1983

PART ONE

HOW TO BE A WARRIOR

༄༅། །ཐེག་པ་ཐམ་མེད་པ་ཡི། །སྲིད་པའི་མེ་ལོང་ཆེན་པོ་ལས།

མི་ཡི་སྲིད་པ་མངོན་པར་དཀར། །དེ་ཚོ་གློག་དང་བཟུལ་བ་བྱུང་།

གདོད་ནས་གྲོལ་བའི་གནི་འཇིང་། །ངོ་ག་སྐྱ་ཞེ་ཚོམ་ཡར་འངེ་ཚོ།

སྤྲ་མའི་ཀྱུ་ཚོགས་དེ་སྐྱེ་དབྱུང་། །གདོད་ནས་གྲོལ་བའི་གནི་བཞི་བཞིང་།

སྐྱོ་ཞིང་རྟེས་སུ་འཛུབ་ལས་བའི་ཚོ། །དཔལ་འབྱོ་བྱུ་ཚོགས་དེ་སྐྱེ་དབྱུང་།

སྤྲ་མའི་ཀྱུ་ཚོགས་མང་པོ་ནི། །ཞག་སྲུག་གགས་སྐྱུང་དག་ཏུ་ཡིན།

སྤུན་ནྲ་བས་ད་གས་སོ་ནས། །ཧྲུའི་གྲོ་རྣམས་ཀྱི་རྟེས་སུ་འཛའ།

གཅིག་གིས་གཅེག་ལ་འཇེགས་སྐྲག་བསྐྱང་། །དེ་ཚོ་ཡར་གློ་ཡར་གིས་བཙ།

ཞེ་སྲུང་མེ་དཔུང་ཆེན་པོ་སྐྱར། །འགོ་ཆགས་ཀྱུ་པོ་ཊག་ཏུ་ཕུར།

ལེ་ལོའི་འདས་ཊབ་འཛ་པར་འཆོ། །ཞད་དང་སྐྱ་གོ་ཞེ་བསྐལ་པ་བྱུང་།

གདོད་མའི་གནི་བ་འཛིང་ལ་ སུས་བའི། དཔལ་འབྱོའི་ཀྱུ་ཚོགས་མང་པོ་རྣམས།

ལ་ལས་མཐིར་དེ་རེ་རོར་ཕྱི། །ཞེ་ལ་སྐྱེ་གནས་མ་ཁྱབ་མཆོག་ལ་བཙེག

ལ་ལ་མཆོ་སྐྱུང་ལ་མཆོ་པར་ཕྱི། །ཡིད་དུ་འོང་བའི་ཕོ་བྲང་བཙེག

ལ་ལ་འདེ་བའི་ཐང་དུ་ཕྱི། །ཞས་འཛས་གྲོ་ཡི་སོ་རྣམ་གནོལ།

ཀུན་ཀྱུང་ཊག་ཏུ་ཚོང་ལ་མེ། །ཊག་ཏུ་ཉམས་ཞེ་གཏང་ཝོང་ཚེ།

མ་བསྐྱལ་པར་བྱུང་སྲུང་སྲུང་གིས། །ཝོང་མ་ཌེགས་སྐྱན་ཊག་ཏུ་སྐུས།

From the great cosmic Mirror
Without beginning and without end,
Human society became manifest.
At that time liberation and confusion arose.
When fear and doubt occurred
Towards the confidence which is primordially free,
Countless multitudes of cowards arose.
When the confidence which is primordially free
Was followed and delighted in,
Countless multitudes of warriors arose.
Those countless multitudes of cowards
Hid themselves in caves and jungles.
They killed their brothers and sisters and ate their flesh,
They followed the example of beasts,
They provoked terror in each other;
Thus they took their own lives.
They kindled a great fire of hatred,
They constantly roiled the river of lust,
They wallowed in the mud of laziness:
The age of famine and plague arose.

Of those who were dedicated to the primordial confidence,
The many hosts of warriors,
Some went to highland mountains
And erected beautiful castles of crystal.
Some went to the lands of beautiful lakes and islands
And erected lovely palaces.
Some went to the pleasant plains
And sowed fields of barley, rice and wheat.
They were always without quarrel,
Ever loving and very generous.
Without encouragement, through their self-existing inscrut-
*   ability,*
They were always devoted to the Imperial Rigden.

ONE

CREATING AN ENLIGHTENED SOCIETY

The Shambhala teachings are founded on the premise that there is basic human wisdom that can help to solve the world's problems. This wisdom does not belong to any one culture or religion, nor does it come only from the West or the East. Rather, it is a tradition of human warriorship that has existed in many cultures at many times throughout history.

IN TIBET, as well as many other Asian countries, there are stories about a legendary kingdom that was a source of learning and culture for present-day Asian societies. According to the legends, this was a place of peace and prosperity, governed by wise and compassionate rulers. The citizens were equally kind and learned, so that, in general, the kingdom was a model society. This place was called Shambhala.

It is said that Buddhism played an important role in the development of the Shambhala society. The legends tell us that Shakyamuni Buddha gave advanced tantric teachings to the first king of Shambhala, Dawa Sangpo. These teachings, which are preserved as the *Kalacakra Tantra,* are considered to be among the most profound wisdom of Tibetan Buddhism. After the king had received this instruction, the stories say that all of the people of Shambhala began to practice meditation and to follow the Buddhist path of loving kindness and concern for all beings. In this way, not just the rulers but

5

all of the subjects of the kingdom became highly developed people.

Among the Tibetan people, there is a popular belief that the kingdom of Shambhala can still be found, hidden in a remote valley somewhere in the Himalayas. There are, as well, a number of Buddhist texts that give detailed but obscure directions for reaching Shambhala, but there are mixed opinions as to whether these should be taken literally or metaphorically. There are also many texts that give us elaborate descriptions of the kingdom. For example, according to the *Great Commentary on the Kalacakra* by the renowned nineteenth-century Buddhist teacher Mipham, the land of Shambhala is north of the river Sita, and the country is divided by eight mountain ranges. The palace of the Rigdens, or the imperial rulers of Shambhala, is built on top of a circular mountain in the center of the country. This mountain, Mipham tells us, is named Kailasa. The palace, which is called the palace of Kalapa, comprises many square miles. In front of it to the south is a beautiful park known as Malaya, and in the middle of the park is a temple devoted to Kalacakra that was built by Dawa Sangpo.

Other legends say that the kingdom of Shambhala disappeared from the earth many centuries ago. At a certain point, the entire society had become enlightened, and the kingdom vanished into another more celestial realm. According to these stories, the Rigden kings of Shambhala continue to watch over human affairs, and will one day return to earth to save humanity from destruction. Many Tibetans believe that the great Tibetan warrior king Gesar of Ling was inspired and guided by the Rigdens and the Shambhala wisdom. This reflects the belief in the celestial existence of the kingdom. Gesar is thought not to have travelled to Shambhala, so his link to the kingdom was a spiritual one. He lived in approximately the eleventh century and ruled the provincial kingdom of Ling, which is located in the province of Kham, East Tibet. Following Gesar's reign, stories about his accomplishments as a warrior and ruler sprang up throughout Tibet, eventually becoming the greatest epic of Tibetan literature. Some legends say that Gesar will reappear from Shambhala, leading an army to conquer the forces of darkness in the world.

In recent years, some Western scholars have suggested that the kingdom of Shambhala may actually have been one of the historically documented kingdoms of early times, such as the Zhang-Zhung kingdom of Central Asia. Many scholars, however, believe that the stories of Shambhala are completely mythical. While it is easy enough to dismiss the kingdom of Shambhala as pure fiction, it is also possible to see in this legend the expression of a deeply rooted and very real human desire for a good and fulfilling life. In fact, among many Tibetan Buddhist teachers, there has long been a tradition that regards the kingdom of Shambhala, not as an external place, but as the ground or root of wakefulness and sanity that exists as a potential within every human being. From that point of view, it is not important to determine whether the kingdom of Shambhala is fact or fiction. Instead, we should appreciate and emulate the ideal of an enlightened society that it represents.

Over the past seven years, I have been presenting a series of "Shambhala teachings" that use the image of the Shambhala kingdom to represent the ideal of secular enlightenment, that is, the possibility of uplifting our personal existence and that of others without the help of any religious outlook. For although the Shambhala tradition is founded on the sanity and gentleness of the Buddhist tradition, at the same time, it has its own independent basis, which is directly cultivating who and what we are as human beings. With the great problems now facing human society, it seems increasingly important to find simple and nonsectarian ways to work with ourselves and to share our understanding with others. The Shambhala teachings or "Shambhala vision," as this approach is more broadly called, is one such attempt to encourage a wholesome existence for ourselves and others.

The current state of world affairs is a source of concern to all of us: the threat of nuclear war, widespread poverty and economic instability, social and political chaos, and psychological upheavals of many kinds. The world is in absolute turmoil. The Shambhala teachings are founded on the premise that there *is* basic human wisdom that can help to solve the world's problems. This wisdom does not belong to any one culture or religion, nor does it come only from the West or the East. Rather, it is a tradition of human warriorship that has existed in many cultures at many times throughout history.

Warriorship here does not refer to making war on others. Aggression is the source of our problems, not the solution. Here the word "warrior" is taken from the Tibetan *pawo*, which literally means "one who is brave." Warriorship in this context is the tradition of human bravery, or the tradition of fearlessness. The North American Indians had such a tradition, and it also existed in South American Indian societies. The Japanese ideal of the samurai also represented a warrior tradition of wisdom, and there have been principles of enlightened warriorship in Western Christian societies as well. King Arthur is a legendary example of warriorship in the Western tradition, and great rulers in the Bible, such as King David, are examples of warriors common to both the Jewish and Christian traditions. On our planet earth there have been many fine examples of warriorship.

The key to warriorship and the first principle of Shambhala vision is not being afraid of who you are. Ultimately, that is the definition of bravery: not being afraid of yourself. Shambhala vision teaches that, in the face of the world's great problems, we can be heroic and kind at the same time. Shambhala vision is the opposite of selfishness. When we are afraid of ourselves and afraid of the seeming threat the world presents, then we become extremely selfish. We want to build our own little nests, our own cocoons, so that we can live by ourselves in a secure way.

But we can be much more brave than that. We must try to think beyond our homes, beyond the fire burning in the fireplace, beyond sending our children to school or getting to work in the morning. We must try to think how we can help this world. If we don't help, nobody will. It is our turn to help the world. At the same time, helping others does not mean abandoning our individual lives. You don't have to rush out to become the mayor of your city or the president of the United States in order to help others, but you can begin with your relatives and friends and the people around you. In fact, you can start with yourself. The important point is to realize

8

that you are never off duty. You can never just relax, because the whole world needs help.

While everyone has a responsibility to help the world, we can create additional chaos if we try to impose our ideas or our help upon others. Many people have theories about what the world needs. Some people think that the world needs communism; some people think that the world needs democracy; some people think that technology will save the world; some people think that technology will destroy the world. The Shambhala teachings are not based on converting the world to another theory. The premise of Shambhala vision is that, in order to establish an enlightened society for others, we need to discover what inherently we have to offer the world. So, to begin with, we should make an effort to examine our own experience, in order to see what it contains that is of value in helping ourselves and others to uplift their existence.

If we are willing to take an unbiased look, we will find that, in spite of all our problems and confusion, all our emotional and psychological ups and downs, there is something basically good about our existence as human beings. Unless we can discover that ground of goodness in our own lives, we cannot hope to improve the lives of others. If we are simply miserable and wretched beings, how can we possibly imagine, let alone realize, an enlightened society?

Discovering real goodness comes from appreciating very simple experiences. We are not talking about how good it feels to make a million dollars or finally graduate from college or buy a new house, but we are speaking here of the basic goodness of being alive—which does not depend on our accomplishments or fulfilling our desires. We experience glimpses of goodness all the time, but we often fail to acknowledge them. When we see a bright color, we are witnessing our own inherent goodness. When we hear a beautiful sound, we are hearing our own basic goodness. When we step out of the shower, we feel fresh and clean, and when we walk out of a stuffy room, we appreciate the sudden whiff of fresh air. These events may take a fraction of a second, but they are real experiences of goodness. They happen to us all the time, but usually we ignore them as mundane or purely coincidental. According to the Shambhala principles, however, it is worthwhile to recognize and take advantage of those moments, because they are revealing basic nonaggression and freshness in our lives—basic goodness.

Every human being has a basic nature of goodness, which is undiluted and unconfused. That goodness contains tremendous gentleness and appreciation. As human beings, we can make love. We can stroke someone with a gentle touch; we can kiss someone with gentle understanding. We can appreciate beauty. We can appreciate the best of this world. We can appreciate its vividness: the yellowness of yellow, the redness of red, the greenness of green, the purpleness of purple. Our experience is real. When yellow is yellow, can we say it is red, if we don't like the yellowness of it? That would be contradicting reality. When we have sunshine, can we reject it and say that the sunshine is terrible? Can we really say that? When we have brilliant sunshine or wonderful snowfall, we appreciate it. And when we appreciate reality, it can actually work on us. We may have to get up in the morning after only a few hours' sleep, but if we look out the window and see the sun shining, it can cheer us up. We can actually cure ourselves of depression if we recognize that the world we have is good.

It is not just an arbitrary idea that the world is good, but it is good because we can *experience* its goodness. We can experience our world as healthy and straightforward, direct and real, because our basic nature is to go along with the goodness of situations. The human potential for intelligence and dignity is attuned to experiencing the brilliance of the bright blue sky, the freshness of green fields, and the beauty of the trees and mountains. We have an actual connection to reality that can wake us up and make us feel basically, fundamentally good. Shambhala vision is tuning in to our ability to wake ourselves up and recognize that goodness can happen to us. In fact, it is happening already.

But then, there is still a question. You might have made a genuine connection to your world: catching a glimpse of sunshine, seeing bright colors, hearing good music, eating good food, or whatever it may be. But how does a glimpse of goodness relate with ongoing experience? On the one hand, you might feel: "I want to get that goodness that is in me and in the phenomenal world." So you rush around trying to find a way to possess it. Or on an even cruder level, you might say: "How much does it cost to get that? That experience was so beautiful. I want to own it." The basic problem with that approach is that you never feel satisfied even if you get what you want, because you still *want* so badly. If you take a walk on Fifth Avenue, you see that kind of desperation. You might say that the people shopping on Fifth Avenue have good taste and that therefore they have possibilities of realizing human dignity. But on the other hand, it is as though they were covered with thorns. They want to grasp more and more and more.

Then, there is the approach of surrendering or humbling yourself to get in touch with goodness. Someone tells you that he can make you happy if you will just give your life to his cause. If you believe that he has the goodness that you want, you may be willing to shave your hair or wear robes or crawl on the floor or eat with your hands to get in touch with goodness. You are willing to trade in your dignity and become a slave.

Both of those situations are attempts to retrieve something good, something real. If you are rich, you are willing to spend thousands of dollars on it. If you are poor, you are willing to commit your life to it. But there is something wrong with both of those approaches.

The problem is that, when we begin to realize the potential goodness in ourselves, we often take our discovery much too seriously. We might kill for goodness or die for goodness; we want it so badly. What is lacking is a sense of humor. Humor here does not mean telling jokes or being comical or criticizing others and laughing at them. A genuine sense of humor is having a light touch: not beating reality into the ground but appreciating reality with a light touch. The basis of Shambhala vision is rediscovering that perfect and real sense of humor, that light touch of appreciation.

If you look at yourself, if you look at your mind, if you look at your activities, you can repossess the humor that you have lost in the course of your life. To begin with, you have to look at your ordinary domestic reality: your knives, your forks, your plates, your telephone, your dishwasher and your towels—ordinary things. There is nothing mystical or extraordinary about them, but if there is no connection with ordinary everyday situations, if you don't examine your mundane life, then you will never find any humor or dignity or, ultimately, any reality.

The way you comb your hair, the way you dress, the way you wash your dishes—all of those activities are an extension of sanity; they are a way of connecting with reality. A fork is a fork, of course. It is a simple implement of eating. But at the same time, the extension of your sanity and your dignity may depend on how you use your fork. Very simply, Shambhala vision is trying to provoke you to understand how you live, you relationship with ordinary life.

As human beings, we are basically awake and we *can* understand reality. We are not enslaved by our lives; we are free. Being free, in this case, means simply that we have a body and a mind, and we can uplift ourselves in order to work with reality in a dignified and humorous way. If we begin to perk up, we will find that the whole universe—including the seasons, the snowfall, the ice and the mud—is also powerfully working with us. Life is a humorous situation, but it is not mocking us. We find that, after all, we can handle our world; we can handle our universe properly and fully in an uplifted fashion.

The discovery of basic goodness is not a religious experience, particularly. Rather it is the realization that we can directly experience and work with reality, the real world that we are in. Experiencing the basic goodness of our lives makes us feel that we are intelligent and decent people and that the world is not a threat. When we feel that our lives are genuine and good, we do not have to deceive ourselves or other people. We can see our shortcomings without feeling guilty or inadequate, and at the same time, we can see our potential for extending goodness to others. We can tell the truth straightforwardly and be absolutely open, but steadfast at the same time.

The essence of warriorship, or the essence of human bravery, is refusing to give up on anyone or anything. We can never say that we are simply falling to pieces or that anyone else is, and we can never say that about the world either. Within our lifetime there will be great problems in the world, but let us make sure that within our lifetime no disasters happen. We can prevent them. It is up to us. We can save the world from destruction, to begin with. That is why Shambhala vision exists. It is a centuries-old idea: by serving this world, we can save it. But saving the world is not enough. We have to work to build an enlightened human society as well.

In this book we are going to discuss the ground of enlightened society and the path towards it, rather than presenting some utopian fantasy of what an enlightened society might be. If we want to help the world, we have to make a personal journey—we can't simply theorize or speculate about our destination. So it is up to each of us individually to find the meaning of enlightened society and how it can be realized. It is my hope that this presentation of the path of the Shambhala warrior may contribute to the dawning of this discovery.

TWO

DISCOVERING BASIC GOODNESS

By simply being on the spot, your life can become workable and even wonderful. You realize that you are capable of sitting like a king or queen on a throne. The regalness of that situation shows you the dignity that comes from being still and simple.

A GREAT DEAL OF CHAOS IN THE WORLD occurs because people don't appreciate themselves. Having never developed sympathy or gentleness towards themselves, they cannot experience harmony or peace within themselves, and therefore, what they project to others is also inharmonious and confused. Instead of appreciating our lives, we often take our existence for granted or we find it depressing and burdensome. People threaten to commit suicide because they aren't getting what they think they deserve out of life. They blackmail others with the threat of suicide, saying that they will kill themselves if certain things don't change. Certainly we should take our lives seriously, but that doesn't mean driving ourselves to the brink of disaster by complaining about our problems or holding a grudge against the world. We have to accept personal responsibility for uplifting our lives.

When you don't punish or condemn yourself, when you relax more and appreciate your body and mind, you begin to contact the fundamental notion of basic goodness in yourself.

14

So it is extremely important to be willing to open yourself to yourself. Developing tenderness towards yourself allows you to see both your problems and your potential accurately. You don't feel that you have to ignore your problems or exaggerate your potential. That kind of gentleness towards yourself and appreciation of yourself is very necessary. It provides the ground for helping yourself and others.

As human beings, we have a working basis within ourselves that allows us to uplift our state of existence and cheer up fully. That working basis is always available to us. We have a mind and a body, which are very precious to us. Because we have a mind and body, we can comprehend this world. Existence is wonderful and precious. We don't know how long we will live, so while we have our life, why not make use of it? Before we even make use of it, why don't we appreciate it?

How do we discover this kind of appreciation? Wishful thinking or simply talking about it does not help. In the Shambhala tradition, the discipline for developing both gentleness towards ourselves and appreciation of our world is the sitting practice of meditation. The practice of meditation was taught by the Lord Buddha over 2,500 years ago, and it has been part of the Shambhala tradition since that time. It is based on an oral tradition: from the time of the Buddha this practice has been transmitted from one human being to another. In this way, it has remained a living tradition, so that, although it is an ancient practice, it is still up to date. In this chapter we are going to discuss the technique of meditation in some detail, but it is important to remember that, if you want to fully understand this practice, you need direct, personal instruction.

By meditation here we mean something very basic and simple that is not tied to any one culture. We are talking about a very basic act: sitting on the ground, assuming a good posture, and developing a sense of our spot, our place on this earth. This is the means of rediscovering ourselves and our basic goodness, the means to tune ourselves in to genuine reality, without any expectations or preconceptions.

The word meditation is sometimes used to mean contemplating a particular theme or object: meditating *on* such and

15

such a thing. By meditating on a question or problem, we can find the solution to it. Sometimes meditation also is connected with achieving a higher state of mind by entering into a trance or absorption state of some kind. But here we are talking about a completely different concept of meditation: unconditional meditation, without any object or idea in mind. In the Shambhala tradition meditation is simply training our state of being so that our mind and body can be synchronized. Through the practice of meditation, we can learn to be without deception, to be fully genuine and alive.

Our life is an endless journey; it is like a broad highway that extends infinitely into the distance. The practice of meditation provides a vehicle to travel on that road. Our journey consists of constant ups and downs, hope and fear, but it is a good journey. The practice of meditation allows us to experience all the textures of the roadway, which is what the journey is all about. Through the practice of meditation, we begin to find that within ourselves there is no fundamental complaint about anything or anyone at all.

Meditation practice begins by sitting down and assuming your seat cross-legged on the ground. You begin to feel that by simply being on the spot, your life can become workable and even wonderful. You realize that you are capable of sitting like a king or queen on a throne. The regalness of that situation shows you the dignity that comes from being still and simple.

In the practice of meditation, an upright posture is extremely important. Having an upright back is not an artificial posture. It is natural to the human body. When you slouch, that is unusual. You can't breathe properly when you slouch, and slouching also is a sign of giving in to neurosis. So when you sit erect, you are proclaiming to yourself and to the rest of the world that you are going to be a warrior, a fully human being.

To have a straight back you do not have to strain yourself by pulling up your shoulders; the uprightness comes naturally from sitting simply but proudly on the ground or on your meditation cushion. Then, because your back is upright, you feel no trace of shyness or embarrassment, so you do not hold your head down. You are not bending to anything.

Because of that, your shoulders become straight automatically, so you develop a good sense of head and shoulders. Then you can allow your legs to rest naturally in a cross-legged position; your knees do not have to touch the ground. You complete your posture by placing your hands lightly, palms down, on your thighs. This provides a further sense of assuming your spot properly.

In that posture, you don't just gaze randomly around. You have a sense that you are *there* properly; therefore your eyes are open, but your gaze is directed slightly downward, maybe six feet in front of you. In that way, your vision does not wander here and there, but you have a further sense of deliberateness and definiteness. You can see this royal pose in some Egyptian and South American sculptures, as well as in Oriental statues. It is a universal posture, not limited to one culture or time.

In your daily life, you should also be aware of your posture, your head and shoulders, how you walk, and how you look at people. Even when you are not meditating, you can maintain a dignified state of existence. You can transcend your embarrassment and take pride in being a human being. Such pride is acceptable and good.

Then, in meditation practice, as you sit with a good posture, you pay attention to your breath. When you breathe, you are utterly there, properly there. You go out with the outbreath, your breath dissolves, and then the inbreath happens naturally. Then you go out again. So there is a constant going out with the outbreath. As you breathe out, you dissolve, you diffuse. Then your inbreath occurs naturally; you don't have to follow it in. You simply come back to your posture, and you are ready for another outbreath. Go out and dissolve: *tshoo;* then come back to your posture; then *tshoo*, and come back to your posture.

Then there will be an inevitable *bing!*—thought. At that point, you say, "thinking." You don't say it out loud; you say it mentally: "thinking." Labelling your thoughts gives you tremendous leverage to come back to your breath. When one thought takes you away completely from what you are actually doing—when you do not even realize that you are on the cushion, but in your mind you are in San Francisco or New

York City—you say "thinking," and you bring yourself back to the breath.

It doesn't really matter what thoughts you have. In the sitting practice of meditation, whether you have monstrous thoughts or benevolent thoughts, all of them are regarded purely as thinking. They are neither virtuous nor sinful. You might have a thought of assassinating your father or you might want to make lemonade and eat cookies. Please don't be shocked by your thoughts: any thought is just thinking. No thought deserves a gold medal or a reprimand. Just label your thoughts "thinking," then go back to your breath. "Thinking," back to the breath; "thinking," back to the breath.

The practice of meditation is very precise. It has to be on the dot, right on the dot. It is quite hard work, but if you remember the importance of your posture, that will allow you to synchronize your mind and body. If you don't have good posture, your practice will be like a lame horse trying to pull a cart. It will never work. So first you sit down and assume your posture, then you work with your breath; *tshoo*, go out, come back to your posture; *tshoo*, come back to your posture; *tshoo*. When thoughts arise, you label them "thinking" and come back to your posture, back to your breath. You have mind working with breath, but you always maintain body as a reference point. You are not working with your mind alone. You are working with your mind and your body, and when the two work together, you never leave reality.

The ideal state of tranquility comes from experiencing body and mind being synchronized. If body and mind are unsynchronized, then your body will slump—and your mind will be somewhere else. It is like a badly made drum: the skin doesn't fit the frame of the drum, so either the frame breaks or the skin breaks, and there is no constant tautness. When mind and body are synchronized, then, because of your good posture, your breathing happens naturally; and because your breathing and your posture work together, your mind has a reference point to check back to. Therefore your mind will go out naturally with the breath.

This method of synchronizing your mind and body is training you to be very simple and to feel that you are not special, but ordinary, extra-ordinary. You sit simply, as a warrior, and out of that, a sense of individual dignity arises. You are sitting on the earth and you realize that this earth deserves you and you deserve this earth. You are there—fully, personally, genuinely. So meditation practice in the Shambhala tradition is designed to educate people to be honest and genuine, true to themselves.

In some sense, we should regard ourselves as being burdened: we have the burden of helping this world. We cannot forget this responsibility to others. But if we take our burden as a delight, we can actually liberate this world. The way to begin is with ourselves. From being open and honest with ourselves, we can also learn to be open with others. So we can work with the rest of the world, on the basis of the goodness we discover in ourselves. Therefore, meditation practice is regarded as a good and in fact excellent way to overcome warfare in the world: our own warfare as well as greater warfare.

THREE

THE GENUINE HEART OF SADNESS

> *Through the practice of sitting still and following your breath as it goes out and dissolves, you are connecting with your heart. By simply letting yourself be, as you are, you develop genuine sympathy towards yourself.*

IMAGINE that you are sitting naked on the ground, with your bare bottom touching the earth. Since you are not wearing a scarf or hat, you are also exposed to heaven above. You are sandwiched between heaven and earth: a naked man or woman, sitting between heaven and earth.

Earth is always earth. The earth will let anyone sit on it, and earth never gives way. It never lets you go—you don't drop off this earth and go flying through outer space. Likewise, sky is always sky; heaven is always heaven above you. Whether it is snowing or raining or the sun is shining, whether it is daytime or nighttime, the sky is always there. In that sense, we know that heaven and earth are trustworthy.

The logic of basic goodness is very similar. When we speak of basic goodness, we are not talking about having allegiance to good and rejecting bad. Basic goodness is good because it is unconditional, or fundamental. It is there already, in the same way that heaven and earth are there already. We don't reject our atmosphere. We don't reject the sun and the moon, the clouds and the sky. We accept them. We accept that the sky is blue; we accept the landscape and the sea. We accept highways and buildings and cities. Basic goodness is that basic, that unconditional. It is not a "for" or "against" view, in the same way that sunlight is not "for" or "against."

The natural law and order of this world is not "for" or "against." Fundamentally, there is nothing that either threatens us or promotes our point of view. The four seasons occur free from anyone's demand or vote. Hope and fear cannot alter the seasons. There is day; there is night. There is darkness at night and light during the day, and no one has to turn a switch on and off. There is a natural law and order that allows us to survive and that is basically good, good in that it is there and it works and it is efficient.

We often take for granted this basic law and order in the universe, but we should think twice. We should appreciate what we have. Without it, we would be in a total predicament. If we didn't have sunlight, we wouldn't have any vegetation, we wouldn't have any crops, and we couldn't cook a meal. So basic goodness is good *because* it is so basic, so fundamental. It is natural and it works, and therefore it is good, rather than being good as opposed to bad.

The same principle applies to our makeup as human beings. We have passion, aggression, and ignorance. That is, we cultivate our friends and we ward off our enemies and we are occasionally indifferent. Those tendencies are not regarded as shortcomings. They are part of the natural elegance and equipment of human beings. We are equipped with nails and teeth to defend ourselves against attack, we are equipped with a mouth and genitals to relate with others, and we are lucky enough to have complete digestive and respiratory systems so that we can process what we take in and flush it out. Human existence is a natural situation, and like the law and order of the world, it is workable and efficient. In fact, it is wonderful, it is ideal.

Some people might say this world is the work of a divine principle, but the Shambhala teachings are not concerned with divine origins. The point of warriorship is to work personally with our situation now, as it is. From the Shambhala point of view, when we say that human beings are basically good, we mean that they have every faculty they need, so that they don't have to fight with their world. Our being is good because it is not a fundamental source of aggression or complaint. We cannot complain that we have eyes, ears, a nose, and a mouth. We cannot redesign our physiological system, and for that matter, we cannot redesign our state of mind. Basic goodness is what we have, what we are provided with. It is the natural situation that we have inherited from birth onwards.

We should feel that it is wonderful to be in this world. How wonderful it is to see red and yellow, blue and green, purple and black! All of these colors are provided for us. We feel hot and cold; we taste sweet and sour. We have these sensations, and we deserve them. They are good.

So the first step in realizing basic goodness is to appreciate what we have. But then we should look further and more precisely at what we are, where we are, who we are, when we are, and how we are as human beings, so that we can take possession of our basic goodness. It is not really a possession, but nonetheless, we deserve it.

Basic goodness is very closely connected to the idea of *bodhicitta* in the Buddhist tradition. *Bodhi* means "awake" or "wakeful" and *citta* means "heart," so *bodhicitta* is "awakened heart." Such awakened heart comes from being willing to face your state of mind. That may seem like a great demand, but it is necessary. You should examine yourself and ask how many times you have tried to connect with your heart, fully and truly. How often have you turned away, because you feared you might discover something terrible about yourself? How often have you been willing to look at your face in the mirror, without being embarrassed? How many times have you tried to shield yourself by reading the newspaper, watching television, or just spacing out? That is the sixty-four-thousand-dollar question: how much have you connected with yourself at all in your whole life?

The sitting practice of meditation, as we discussed in the last chapter, is the means to rediscover basic goodness, and beyond that, it is the means to awaken this genuine heart within yourself. When you sit in the posture of meditation, you are exactly the naked man or woman that we described earlier, sitting between heaven and earth. When you slouch, you are trying to hide your heart, trying to protect it by slumping over. But when vou sit upright but relaxed in the posture of meditation, your heart is naked. Your entire being is exposed—to yourself, first of all, but to others as well. So through the practice of sitting still and following your breath as it goes out and dissolves, you are connecting with your heart. By simply letting yourself be, as you are, you develop genuine sympathy towards yourself.

When you awaken your heart in this way, you find, to your surprise, that your heart is empty. You find that you are looking into outer space. What are you, who are you, where is your heart? If you really look, you won't find anything tangible and solid. Of course, you might find something *very* solid if you have a grudge against someone or you have fallen possessively in love. But that is not awakened heart. If you search for awakened heart, if you put your hand through your rib cage and feel for it, there is nothing there except for tenderness. You feel sore and soft, and if you open your eyes to the rest of the world, you feel tremendous sadness. This kind of sadness doesn't come from being mistreated. You don't feel sad because someone has insulted you or because you feel impoverished. Rather, this experience of sadness is unconditioned. It occurs because your heart is completely exposed. There is no skin or tissue covering it; it is pure raw meat. Even if a tiny mosquito lands on it, you feel so touched. Your experience is raw and tender and so personal.

The genuine heart of sadness comes from feeling that your nonexistent heart is full. You would like to spill your heart's blood, give your heart to others. For the warrior, this experience of sad and tender heart is what gives birth to fearlessness. Conventionally, being fearless means that you are not afraid or that, if someone hits you, you will hit him back. However, we are not talking about that street-fighter level of fearlessness. Real fearlessness is the product of tenderness. It comes from letting the world tickle your heart, your raw and beautiful heart. You are willing to open up, without resistance or shyness, and face the world. You are willing to share your heart with others.

FOUR

FEAR AND FEARLESSNESS

> *Acknowledging fear is not a cause for depression or discouragement. Because we possess such fear, we also are potentially entitled to experience fearlessness. True fearlessness is not the reduction of fear, but going beyond fear.*

IN ORDER TO EXPERIENCE FEARLESSNESS, it is necessary to experience fear. The essence of cowardice is not acknowledging the reality of fear. Fear can take many forms. Logically, we know we can't live forever. We know that we are going to die, so we are afraid. We are petrified of our death. On another level, we are afraid that we can't handle the demands of the world. This fear expresses itself as a feeling of inadequacy. We feel that our own lives are overwhelming, and confronting the rest of the world is more overwhelming. Then there is abrupt fear, or panic, that arises when new situations occur suddenly in our lives. When we feel that we can't handle them, we jump or twitch. Sometimes fear manifests in the form of restlessness: doodles on a note pad, playing with our fingers, or fidgeting in our chairs. We feel that we have to keep ourselves moving all the time, like an engine running in a motor car. The pistons go up and down, up and down. As long as the pistons keep moving, we feel safe. Otherwise, we are afraid we might die on the spot.

There are innumerable strategies that we use to take our minds off of fear. Some people take tranquilizers. Some people do yoga. Some people watch television or read a magazine or go to a bar to have a beer. From the coward's point of view, boredom should be avoided, because when we are bored we begin to feel anxious. We are getting closer to our fear. Entertainment should be promoted and any thought of death should be avoided. So cowardice is trying to live our lives as though death were unknown. There have been periods in history in which many people searched for a potion of longevity. If there were such a thing, most people would find it quite horrific. If they had to live in this world for a thousand years without dying, long before they got to their thousandth birthday, they would probably commit suicide. Even if you could live forever, you would be unable to avoid the reality of death and suffering around you.

Fear has to be acknowledged. We have to realize our fear and reconcile ourselves with fear. We should look at how we move, how we talk, how we conduct ourselves, how we chew our nails, how we sometimes put our hands in our pockets uselessly. Then we will find something out about how fear is expressed in the form of restlessness. We must face the fact that fear is lurking in our lives, always, in everything we do.

On the other hand, acknowledging fear is not a cause for depression or discouragement. Because we possess such fear, we also are potentially entitled to experience fearlessness. True fearlessness is not the reduction of fear, but going beyond fear. Unfortunately, in the English language, we don't have one word that means that. Fearlessness is the closest term, but by fear*less* we don't mean "less fear," but "beyond fear."

Going beyond fear begins when we examine our fear: our anxiety, nervousness, concern, and restlessness. If we look into our fear, if we look beneath its veneer, the first thing we find is sadness, beneath the nervousness. Nervousness is cranking up, vibrating, all the time. When we slow down, when we relax with our fear, we find sadness, which is calm and gentle. Sadness hits you in your heart, and your body produces a tear. Before you cry, there is a feeling in

25

your chest and then, after that, you produce tears in your eyes. You are about to produce rain or a waterfall in your eyes and you feel sad and lonely, and perhaps romantic at the same time. That is the first tip of fearlessness, and the first sign of real warriorship. You might think that, when you experience fearlessness, you will hear the opening to Beethoven's Fifth Symphony or see a great explosion in the sky, but it doesn't happen that way. In the Shambhala tradition, discovering fearlessness comes from working with the softness of the human heart.

The birth of the warrior is like the first growth of a reindeer's horns. At first, the horns are very soft and almost rubbery, and they have little hairs growing on them. They are not yet horns, as such: they are just sloppy growths with blood inside. Then, as the reindeer ages, the horns grow stronger, developing four points or ten points or even forty points. Fearlessness, at the beginning, is like those rubbery horns. They look like horns, but you can't quite fight with them. When a reindeer first grows its horns, it doesn't know what to use them for. It must feel very awkward to have those soft, lumpy growths on your head. But then the reindeer begins to realize that it *should* have horns: that horns are a natural part of being a reindeer. In the same way, when a human being first gives birth to the tender heart of warriorship, he or she may feel extremely awkward or uncertain about how to relate to this kind of fearlessness. But then, as you experience this sadness more and more, you realize that human beings *should* be tender and open. So you no longer need to feel shy or embarrassed about being gentle. In fact, your softness begins to become passionate. You would like to extend yourself to others and communicate with them.

When tenderness evolves in that direction, then you can truly appreciate the world around you. Sense perceptions become very interesting things. You are so tender and open already that you cannot help opening yourself to what takes place all around you. When you see red or green or yellow or black, you respond to them from the bottom of your heart. When you see someone else crying or laughing or being afraid, you respond to them as well. At that point, your beginning level of fearlessness is developing further into

26

warriorship. When you begin to feel comfortable being a gentle and decent person, your reindeer horns no longer have little hairs growing on them—they are becoming real horns. Situations become very real, quite real, and on the other hand, quite ordinary. Fear evolves into fearlessness naturally, very simply, and quite straightforwardly.

The ideal of warriorship is that the warrior should be sad and tender, and because of that, the warrior can be very brave as well. Without that heartfelt sadness, bravery is brittle, like a china cup. If you drop it, it will break or chip. But the bravery of the warrior is like a lacquer cup, which has a wooden base covered with layers of lacquer. If the cup drops, it will bounce rather than break. It is soft and hard at the same time.

FIVE

SYNCHRONIZING MIND AND BODY

Synchronizing mind and body is not a concept or a random technique someone thought up for self-improvement. Rather, it is a basic principle of how to be a human being and how to use your sense perceptions, your mind and your body together.

THE EXPRESSION OF BASIC GOODNESS is always connected with gentleness—not feeble, lukewarm, milk-and-honey gentleness, but wholehearted, perky gentleness with good head and shoulders. Gentleness, in this sense, comes from experiencing the absence of doubt, or doubtlessness. Being without doubt has nothing to do with accepting the validity of a philosophy or concept. It is not that you should be converted or subjected to someone's crusade until you have no doubt about your beliefs. We are not talking about doubtless people who become evangelical crusaders, ready to sacrifice themselves for their beliefs. Absence of doubt is trusting in the heart, trusting yourself. Being without doubt means that you have connected with yourself, that you have experienced mind and body being synchronized together. When mind and body are synchronized, then you have no doubt.

Synchronizing mind and body is not a concept or a random technique someone thought up for self-improvement. Rather, it is a basic principle of how to be a human being and

28

how to use your sense perceptions, your mind and your body together. The body can be likened to a camera, and the mind to the film inside the camera. The question is how you can use them together. When the aperture and the shutter speed of the camera are properly set, in relation to the speed of the film inside the camera, then you can take good, accurate photographs, because you have synchronized the camera and the film. Similarly, when mind and body are properly synchronized, then you have clear perception and you have a sense of being without doubt, being without the tremors and the shaking and the shortsightedness of anxiety, which make your behavior totally inaccurate.

When body and mind are not synchronized, sometimes your mind is short and your body is long, or sometimes your mind is long and your body is short. So you are uncertain about how to even pick up a glass of water. Sometimes you reach too far, and sometimes you don't reach far enough, and you can't get hold of your water glass. When mind and body are unsynchronized, then, if you are doing archery, you can't hit the target. If you are doing calligraphy, you can't even dip your brush into the inkwell, let alone make a brushstroke.

Synchronizing mind and body is also connected with how we synchronize or connect with the world, how we work with the world altogether. This process has two stages, which we could call looking and seeing. We might also speak of listening and hearing, or touching and then feeling, but it is somewhat easier to explain this process of synchronization in terms of visual perception. Looking is your first projection, and if you have any doubt, then it might have a quality of tremor or shakiness. You begin to look, and then you feel shaky or anxious because you don't trust your vision. So sometimes you want to close your eyes. You don't want to look any more. But the point is to look properly. See the colors: white, black, blue, yellow, red, green, purple. Look. This is your world! You can't not look. There is no other world. This is your world; it is your feast. You inherited this; you inherited these eyeballs; you inherited this world of color. Look at the greatness of the whole thing. Look! Don't hesitate—look! Open your eyes. Don't blink, and look, look— look further.

Then you might *see* something, which is the second stage. The more you look, the more inquisitive you are, the more you are bound to see. Your looking process is not restrained, because you are genuine, you are gentle, you have nothing to lose, and you have nothing to fight against. You can look so much, you can look further, and then you can see so beautifully. In fact, you can feel the warmth of red and the coolness of blue and the richness of yellow and the penetrating quality of green—all at once. You appreciate the world around you. It is a fantastic new discovery of the world. You would like to explore the entire universe.

Sometimes, when we perceive the world, we perceive without language. We perceive spontaneously, with a pre-language system. But sometimes when we view the world, first we think a word and then we perceive. In other words, the first instance is directly feeling or perceiving the universe; the second is talking ourselves into seeing our universe. So either you look and see beyond language—as first perception—or you see the world through the filter of your thoughts, by talking to yourself. Everyone knows what it is like to feel things directly. Intense emotion—passion and aggression and jealousy—don't have a language. They are too intense in the first flash. After that first flash, then you begin to think in your mind: "I hate you" or "I love you" or you say, "Should I love you so much?" A little conversation takes place in your mind.

Synchronizing mind and body is looking and seeing directly beyond language. This is not because of a disrespect for language but because your internal dialogue becomes subconscious gossip. You develop your own poetry and daydreams; you develop your own swear words; and you begin to have conversations between you and yourself and your lover and your teacher—all in your mind. On the other hand, when you feel that you can afford to relax and perceive the world directly, then your vision can expand. You can see on the spot with wakefulness. Your eyes begin to open, wider and wider, and you see that the world is colorful and fresh and so precise; every sharp angle is fantastic.

In that way, synchronizing mind and body is also connected with developing fearlessness. By fearlessness, we do not mean that you are willing to jump off a cliff or to put your naked finger on a hot stove. Rather, here fearlessness means being able to respond accurately to the phenomenal world altogether. It simply means being accurate and absolutely direct in relating with the phenomenal world by means of your sense perceptions, your mind, and your sense of vision. That fearless vision reflects on you as well: it affects how you see yourself. If you look at yourself in the mirror—at your hair, your teeth, your moustache, your coat, your shirt, your tie, your dress, your pearls, your earrings—you see that they all belong there and that you belong there, as you are. You begin to realize that you have a perfect right to be in this universe, to be this way, and you see that there is a basic hospitality that this world provides to you. You have looked and you have seen, and you don't have to apologize for being born on this earth.

This discovery is the first glimpse of what is called the Great Eastern Sun. When we say sun here, we mean the sun of human dignity, the sun of human power. The Great Eastern Sun is a rising sun rather than a setting sun, so it represents the dawning, or awakening of human dignity—the rising of human warriorship. Synchronizing mind and body brings the dawn of the Great Eastern Sun.

SIX

THE DAWN OF THE GREAT EASTERN SUN

The way of the Great Eastern Sun is based on see-ing that there is a natural source of radiance and brilliance in this world—which is the innate wake-fulness of human beings.

THE DAWN OF THE GREAT EASTERN SUN is based on actual experience. It is not a concept. You realize that you can uplift yourself, that you can appreciate your existence as a human being. Whether you are a gas station attendant or the president of your country doesn't really matter. When you experience the goodness of being alive, you can respect who and what you are. You need not be intimidated by lots of bills to pay, diapers to change, food to cook, or papers to be filed. Fundamentally, in spite of all those responsibilities, you begin to feel that it is a worthwhile situation to be a human being, to be alive, not afraid of death.

Death comes, obviously. You can never avoid death. Whatever you do, death occurs. But if you have lived with a sense of reality and with gratitude towards life, then you leave the dignity of your life behind you, so that your relatives, your friends, and your children can appreciate who you were. The vision of the Great Eastern Sun is based on celebrating life. It is contrasted to the setting sun, the sun that is going down and dissolving into darkness. The setting-sun vision is based on trying to ward off the concept of death, trying to save ourselves from dying. The setting-sun point of view is based on fear. We are constantly afraid of ourselves. We feel that we can't actually hold ourselves upright. We are so ashamed of ourselves, who we are, what we are. We are ashamed of our jobs, our finances, our parental upbringing, our education, and our psychological shortcomings.

Great Eastern Sun vision, on the other hand, is based on appreciating ourselves and appreciating our world, so it is a very gentle approach. Because we appreciate the world, we don't make a mess in it. We take care of our bodies, we take care of our minds, and we take care of our world. The world around us is regarded as very sacred, so we have to constantly serve our world and clean it up. The setting-sun vision is that washing things and cleaning up should be the domain of hired help. Or if you can't afford a housekeeper, you clean up yourself, but you regard it as dirty work. Having a nice meal is fine, but who is going to wash the dishes? We would prefer to leave that to someone else.

Thousands of tons of leftovers are discarded every year. When people go to restaurants, often they are served giant platefuls of food, more than they can eat, to satisfy the giant desire of their minds. Their minds are stuffed just by the visual appearance of their giant steaks, their full plates. Then the leftovers are thrown into the garbage. All that food is wasted, absolutely wasted.

That is indeed a setting-sun approach. You have a giant vision, which you can't consume, and you end up throwing most of it away. There is not even a program to recycle the leftovers. Everything goes to the dump. It is no wonder we have such big problems disposing of our garbage. Some people have even thought of sending our garbage into outer space: we can let the rest of the universe take care of our leftovers, instead of cleaning up our earth. The setting-sun approach is to shield ourselves from dirt as much as we can, so that we don't have to look at it—we just get rid of anything unpleasant. As long as we have a pleasurable situation, we forget about the leftovers or the greasy spoons and plates. We leave the job of cleaning up to somebody else.

33

That approach produces an oppressive social hierarchy in the setting-sun world: there are those who get rid of other people's dirt and those who take pleasure in producing the dirt. Those people who have money can continue to enjoy their food and ignore the leftovers. They can pay for luxury and ignore reality. In that way of doing things, you never see the dirt properly, and you may never see the food properly, either. Everything is compartmentalized, so you can never experience things completely. We are not talking purely about food; we are talking about everything that goes on in the setting-sun world: packaged food, packaged vacations, package deals of all kinds. There is no room to experience doubtlessness in that world; there is no room to be gentle; there is no room to experience reality fully and properly.

In contrast to that, Great Eastern Sun vision is a very ecological approach. The way of the Great Eastern Sun is based on seeing what is needed and how things happen organically. So the sense of hierarchy, or order, in the Great Eastern Sun world is not connected with imposing arbitrary boundaries or divisions. Great Eastern Sun hierarchy comes from seeing life as a natural process and tuning in to the uncontrived order that exists in the world. Great Eastern Sun hierarchy is based on seeing that there is a natural source of radiance and brilliance in this world—which is the innate wakefulness of human beings. The sun of human dignity can be likened to the physical sun spanning the darkness. When you have a brilliant sun, which is a source of vision, the light from the sun shines through every window of the house, and the brightness of its light inspires you to open all the curtains. The analogy for hierarchy in the Great Eastern Sun world is a flowering plant that grows upwards towards the sun. The analogy for setting-sun hierarchy is a lid that flattens you and keeps you in your place. In the vision of the Great Eastern Sun, even criminals can be cultivated, encouraged to grow up. In the setting-sun vision, criminals are hopeless, so they are shut off; they don't have a chance. They are part of the dirt that we would rather not see. But in the vision of the Great Eastern Sun, no human being is a lost cause. We don't feel that we have to put a lid on anyone or anything. We are always willing to give things a chance to flower.

The basis of Great Eastern Sun vision is realizing that the world is clean and pure to begin with. There is no problem with cleaning things up, if we realize that we are just returning them to their natural, original state. It is like having your teeth cleaned. When you leave the dentist's office, your teeth feel so good. You feel as though you had a new set of teeth, but in actual fact, it is just that your teeth are clean. You realize that they are basically good teeth.

35

In working with ourselves, cleaning up begins by telling the truth. We have to shed any hesitation about being honest with ourselves because it might be unpleasant. If you feel bad when you come home because you had a hard day at the office, you can tell the truth about that: you feel bad. Then you don't have to try to shake off your pain by throwing it around your living room. Instead, you can start to relax; you can be genuine at home. You can take a shower and put on fresh clothes and take some refreshment. You can change your shoes, go outside, and walk in your garden. Then, you might feel better. In fact, when you get close to the truth, you can tell the truth and feel great.

In this world, there are always possibilities of original purity, because the world is clean to begin with. Dirt never comes first, at all. For example, when you buy new towels, they don't have any dirt on them. Then, as you use them, they become dirty. But you can always wash them and return them to their original state. In the same way, our entire physical and psychological existence and the world that we know—our sky, our earth, our houses, everything we have—was and is originally clean. But then, we begin to smear the situation with our conflicting emotions. Still, fundamentally speaking, our existence is all good, and it is all launderable. That is what we mean by basic goodness: the pure ground that is always there, waiting to be cleaned by us. We can always return to that primordial ground. That is the logic of the Great Eastern Sun.

SEVEN

THE COCOON

> *The way of cowardice is to embed ourselves in a co-coon, in which we perpetuate our habitual patterns. When we are constantly recreating our basic patterns of behavior and thought, we never have to leap into fresh air or onto fresh ground.*

IN THE LAST CHAPTER we talked about the dawn of the Great Eastern Sun. However, in general, we are much more accustomed to the darkness of the setting-sun world than we are to the light of the Great Eastern Sun. Therefore, our next topic is dealing with darkness. By darkness, we mean enclosing ourselves in a familiar world in which we can hide or go to sleep. It is as though we would like to re-enter our mother's womb and hide there forever, so that we could avoid being born. When we are afraid of waking up and afraid of experiencing our own fear, we create a cocoon to shield ourselves from the vision of the Great Eastern Sun. We prefer to hide in our personal jungles and caves. When we hide from the world in this way, we feel secure. We may think that we have quieted our fear, but we are actually making ourselves numb with fear. We surround ourselves with our own familiar thoughts, so that nothing sharp or painful can touch us. We are so afraid of our own fear that we deaden our hearts.

The way of cowardice is to embed ourselves in this cocoon, in which we perpetuate our habitual patterns. When we are constantly recreating our basic patterns of behavior and thought, we never have to leap into fresh air or onto fresh ground. Instead, we wrap ourselves in our own dark environment, where our only companion is the smell of our own sweat. We regard this dank cocoon as a family heirloom or inheritance, and we don't want to give that bad-good, good-bad memory away. In the cocoon there is no dance: no walking, or breathing, not even a wink of the eyes. It is comfortable and sleepy: an intense and very familiar home. In the world of the cocoon, such things as spring cleaning have never been known. We feel that it is too much work, too much trouble, to clean it up. We would prefer to go back to sleep.

In the cocoon there is no idea of light at all, until we experience some longing for openness, some longing for something other than the smell of our own sweat. When we begin to examine that comfortable darkness—look at it, smell it, feel it—we find it is claustrophobic. So the first impulse that draws us away from the darkness of the cocoon towards the light of the Great Eastern Sun is a longing for ventilation. As soon as we begin to sense the possibility of fresh air, we realize that our arms and legs are being restricted. We want to stretch out and walk, dance, even jump. We realize that there is an alternative to our cocoon: we discover that we could be free from that trap. With that longing for fresh air, for a breeze of delight, we open our eyes, and we begin to look for an alternative environment to our cocoon. And to our surprise, we begin to see light, even though it may be hazy at first. The tearing of the cocoon takes place at that point.

Then we realize that the degraded cocoon we have been hiding in is revolting, and we want to turn up the lights as far as we can. In fact, we are not turning up the lights, but we are simply opening our eyes wider: constantly looking for the brightest light. So we catch a certain kind of fever: the fever of the Great Eastern Sun. But again and again, we should reflect back to the darkness of the cocoon. In order to inspire ourselves to move forward, we must look back to see the contrast with the place we came from.

If we don't look back, then we will have difficulty relating to the reality of the setting sun. You see, we cannot just reject the world of the cocoon, even though it is quite horrific and unnecessary. We have to develop genuine sympathy for our own experiences of darkness as well as those of others. Otherwise, our journey out of the cocoon simply becomes a setting-sun holiday. Without the reference point of looking back, we have a tendency to create a new cocoon in the Great Eastern Sun. Now that we have left the darkness behind, we feel that we can just bathe in the sun, lying in the sand and stupefying ourselves.

But when we look back to the cocoon and see the suffering that takes place in the world of the coward, that inspires us to go forward in our journey of warriorship. It is not a journey in the sense of walking in the desert looking ahead to the horizon. Rather, it is a journey that is unfolding within us. So, we begin to appreciate the Great Eastern Sun, not as something outside of us, like the sun in the sky, but as the Great Eastern Sun in our head and shoulders, in our face, our hair, our lips, our chest. If we examine our posture, our behavior, our existence, we find that the attributes of the Great Eastern Sun are reflected in every aspect of our being.

This brings a feeling of being a truly human being. Physically, psychologically, domestically, spiritually, we feel that we can lead our lives in the fullest way. There is a gut-level sense of health and wholesomeness taking place in our lives, as if we were holding a solid brick of gold. It is heavy and full, and it shines with a golden color. There is something very real and, at the same time, very rich about our human existence. Out of that feeling, a tremendous sense of health can be propagated to others. In fact, propagating health to our world becomes a basic discipline of warriorship. By discipline we do not mean something unpleasant or artificial that is imposed from outside. Rather, this discipline is an organic process that expands naturally from our own experience. When we feel healthy and wholesome ourselves, then we cannot help projecting that healthiness to others.

Great Eastern Sun vision brings natural interest in the world outside. Ordinarily, "interest" occurs when something extraordinary happens and makes you "interested" in it. Or being interested may come from being bored, so you find interests to occupy your time. Interest also occurs when you feel threatened. You become very inquisitive and sharp in order to protect yourself, so that nothing terrible will happen. For the warrior, interest happens spontaneously because there is already so much health and togetherness taking place in his or her life. The warrior feels that the world is naturally full of interest: the visual world, the emotional world, whatever world he might have. So interest or inquisitiveness manifests as raw delight, delight together with rawness or tenderness.

Usually when you are delighted about something, you develop a thick skin, and you feel smug. You say to yourself, "I'm so delighted to be here." That is just self-affirmation. But in this case, delight has a touch of pain to it, because you feel sore or raw in relation to your world. In fact, tenderness and sadness, as well as gentleness, actually produce a sense of interest. You are so vulnerable that you cannot help being touched by your world. That is a sort of saving grace, or safety precaution, so that the warrior never goes astray and never grows a thick skin. Whenever there is interest, the warrior also reflects back to the sadness, the tenderness, which projects further genuineness and sparks further interest.

The Great Eastern Sun illuminates the way of discipline for the warrior. An analogy for that is the beams of light you see when you look at the sunrise. The rays of light coming towards you almost seem to provide a pathway for you to walk on. In the same way, the Great Eastern Sun creates an atmosphere in which you can constantly move forward, recharging energy all the time. Your whole life is constantly moving forward, even though you may be doing something quite repetitive, such as working in a factory or at a hamburger stand. Whatever you may be doing, every minute of every hour is a new chapter, a new page. A warrior doesn't need color television or video games. A warrior doesn't need to read comic books to entertain himself or to be cheerful. The world that goes on around the warrior is what it is, and in that world the question of entertainment doesn't arise. So the Great Eastern Sun provides the means to take advantage of your life in the fullest way. Then you find that you don't have to ask an architect or a tailor to redesign your world for you. At the point of realizing that, a further sense of warriorship can take place: becoming a real warrior.

For the true warrior, there is no warfare. This is the idea of being all-victorious. When you are all-victorious, there is nothing to conquer, no fundamental problem or obstacle to overcome. This attitude is not based on suppressing or overlooking negativity, particularly. But if you look back and trace back through your life—who you are, what you are, and why you are in this world—if you look through that step-by-step, you won't find any fundamental problems.

This is not a matter of talking yourself into believing that everything is okay. Rather, if you actually look, if you take your whole being apart and examine it, you find that you are genuine and good as you are. In fact, the whole of existence is well-constructed, so that there is very little room for mishaps of any kind. There are, of course, constant challenges, but the sense of challenge is quite different from the setting-sun feeling that you are condemned to your world and your problems. Occasionally people are frightened by this vision of the Great Eastern Sun. Not knowing the nature of fear, of course, you cannot go beyond it. But once you know your cowardice, once you know where the stumbling block is, you can climb over it—maybe just three-and-a-half steps.

EIGHT

RENUNCIATION AND DARING

What the warrior renounces is anything in his experience that is a barrier between himself and others. In other words, renunciation is making yourself more available, more gentle and open to others.

THE SITUATIONS OF FEAR that exist in our lives provide us with stepping stones to step over our fear. On the other side of cowardice is bravery. If we step over properly, we can cross the boundary from being cowardly to being brave. We may not discover bravery right away. Instead, we may find a shaky tenderness beyond our fear. We are still quivering and shaking, but there is tenderness, rather than bewilderment.

Tenderness contains an element of sadness, as we have discussed. It is not the sadness of feeling sorry for yourself or feeling deprived, but it is a natural situation of fullness. You feel so full and rich, as if you were about to shed tears. Your eyes are full of tears, and the moment you blink, the tears will spill out of your eyes and roll down your cheeks. In order to be a good warrior, one has to feel this sad and tender heart. If a person does not feel alone and sad, he cannot be a warrior at all. The warrior is sensitive to every aspect of phenomena—sight, smell, sound, feelings. He appreciates everything that goes on in his world as an artist does. His experience is full and extremely vivid. The rustling of leaves and the sounds of raindrops on his coat are very loud. Occasional butterflies fluttering around him may be almost unbearable because he is so sensitive. Because of his sensitivity, the warrior can then go further in developing his discipline. He begins to learn the meaning of renunciation.

In the ordinary sense, renunciation is often connected with asceticism. You give up the sense pleasures of the world and embrace an austere spiritual life in order to understand the higher meaning of existence. In the Shambhala context, renunciation is quite different. What the warrior renounces is anything in his experience that is a barrier between himself and others. In other words, renunciation is making yourself more available, more gentle and open to others. Any hesitation about opening yourself to others is removed. For the sake of others, you renounce your privacy.

The need for renunciation arises when you begin to feel that basic goodness belongs to you. Of course, you cannot make a personal possession out of basic goodness. It is the law and order of the world, which is impossible to possess personally. It is a greater vision, much greater than your personal territory or schemes. Nonetheless, sometimes you try to localize basic goodness in yourself. You think that you can take a little pinch of basic goodness and keep it in your pocket. So the idea of privacy begins to creep in. That is the point at which you need renunciation—renunciation of the temptation to possess basic goodness. It is necessary to give up a localized approach, a provincial approach, and to accept a greater world.

Renunciation also is necessary if you are frightened by the vision of the Great Eastern Sun. When you realize how vast and good the Great Eastern Sun is, sometimes you feel overwhelmed. You feel that you need a little shelter from it, a roof over your head and three square meals a day. You try to build a little nest, a little home, to contain or limit what you have seen. It seems too vast, so you would like to take photographs of the Great Eastern Sun and keep them as a memory, rather than staring directly into the light. The principle of renunciation is to reject any small-mindedness of that kind.

The sitting practice of meditation provides an ideal environment to develop renunciation. In meditation, as you work with your breath, you regard any thoughts that arise as just your thinking process. You don't hold on to any thought and you don't have to punish your thoughts or praise them. The thoughts that occur during sitting practice are regarded as natural events, but at the same time, they don't carry any credentials. The basic definition of meditation is "having a steady mind." In meditation, when your thoughts go up, you don't go up, and you don't go down when your thoughts go down; you just watch as thoughts go up and thoughts go down. Whether your thoughts are good or bad, exciting or boring, blissful or miserable, you let them be. You don't accept some and reject others. You have a sense of greater space that encompasses any thought that may arise.

In other words, in meditation you can experience a sense of existence, or being, that includes your thoughts but is not conditioned by your thoughts or limited to your thinking process. You experience your thoughts, you label them "thinking," and you come back to your breath, going out, expanding, and dissolving into space. It is very simple, but it is quite profound. You experience your world directly and you do not have to limit that experience. You can be completely open, with nothing to defend and nothing to fear. In that way, you are developing renunciation of personal territory and small-mindedness.

At the same time, renunciation does involve discrimination. Within the basic context of openness there is a discipline of what to ward off, or reject, and what to cultivate, or accept. The positive aspect of renunciation, what is cultivated, is caring for others. But in order to care for others, it is necessary to reject caring only for yourself, or the attitude of selfishness. A selfish person is like a turtle carrying its home on its back wherever it goes. At some point you have to leave home and embrace a larger world. That is the absolute prerequisite for being able to care for others.

In order to overcome selfishness, it is necessary to be daring. It is as though you were dressed in your swimsuit, standing on the diving board with a pool in front of you, and you ask yourself: "Now what?" The obvious answer is: "Jump."

That is daring. You might wonder if you will sink or hurt yourself if you jump. You might. There is no insurance, but it is worthwhile jumping to find out what will happen. The student warrior has to jump. We are so accustomed to accepting what is bad for us and rejecting what is good for us. We are attracted to our cocoons, our selfishness, and we are afraid of selflessness, stepping beyond ourselves. So in order to overcome our hesitation about giving up our privacy, and in order to commit ourselves to others' welfare, some kind of leap is necessary.

In the practice of meditation, the way to be daring, the way to leap, is to disown your thoughts, to step beyond your hope and fear, the ups and downs of your thinking process. You can just be, just let yourself be, without holding on to the constant reference points that mind manufactures. You do not have to get rid of your thoughts. They are a natural process; they are fine; let them be as well. But let yourself go out with the breath, let it dissolve. See what happens. When you let yourself go in that way, you develop trust in the strength of your being and trust in your ability to open and extend yourself to others. You realize that you are rich and resourceful enough to give selflessly to others, and as well, you find that you have tremendous willingness to do so.

But then, once you have made a leap of daring, you might become arrogant. You might say to yourself: "Look, I have jumped! I am so great, so fantastic!" But arrogant warriorship does not work. It does nothing to benefit others. So the discipline of renunciation also involves cultivating further gentleness, so that you remain very soft and open and allow tenderness to come into your heart. The warrior who has accomplished true renunciation is completely naked and raw, without even skin or tissue. He has renounced putting on a new suit of armor or growing a thick skin, so his bone and marrow are exposed to the world. He has no room and no desire to manipulate situations. He is able to be, quite fearlessly, what he is.

At this point, having completely renounced his own comfort and privacy, paradoxically, the warrior finds himself more alone. He is like an island sitting alone in the middle of a lake. Occasional ferry boats and commuters go back and forth between the shore and the island, but all that activity only expresses the further loneliness, or the aloneness, of the island. Although the warrior's life is dedicated to helping others, he realizes that he will never be able to completely share his experience with others. The fullness of his experience is his own, and he must live with his own truth. Yet he is more and more in love with the world. That combination of love affair and loneliness is what enables the warrior to constantly reach out to help others. By renouncing his private world, the warrior discovers a greater universe and a fuller and fuller broken heart. This is not something to feel bad about: it is a cause for rejoicing. It is entering the warrior's world.

NINE

CELEBRATING THE JOURNEY

Warriorship is a continual journey. To be a warrior is to learn to be genuine in every moment of your life.

THE GOAL OF WARRIORSHIP is to express basic goodness in its most complete, fresh, and brilliant form. This is possible when you realize that you do not *possess* basic goodness but that you *are* the basic goodness itself. Therefore, training yourself to be a warrior is learning to rest in basic goodness, to rest in a complete state of simplicity. In the Buddhist tradition, that state of being is called *egolessness*. Egolessness is also very important to the Shambhala teachings. It is impossible to be a warrior unless you have experienced egolessness. Without egolessness, your mind will be filled with your self, your personal projects and schemes. Instead of concern for others, you become preoccupied with your own "egofulness." The colloquial expression that someone is "full of himself" refers to this kind of arrogance and false pride.

Renunciation, as discussed in the last chapter, is the attitude that overcomes selfishness. The result of renunciation is that you enter the warrior's world, a world in which you are more available and open to others, but also more brokenhearted and alone. You begin to understand that warriorship is a path or a thread that runs through your entire life. It is not just a technique that you apply when an obstacle arises or when you are unhappy or depressed. Warriorship is a continual journey. To be a warrior is to learn to be genuine in every moment of your life. That is the warrior's discipline.

There are, unfortunately, many negative connotations of the word "discipline." Discipline is often associated with punishment, imposing arbitrary rules and authority, or control. In the Shambhala tradition, however, discipline is connected with how to become thoroughly gentle and genuine. It is associated with how to overcome selfishness and how to promote egolessness, or basic goodness, in yourself and others. Discipline shows you how to make the journey of warriorship. It guides you in the way of the warrior and shows you how to live in the warrior's world.

The warrior's discipline is unwavering and all-pervasive. Therefore, it is like the sun. The light of the sun shines wherever the sun rises. The sun does not decide to shine on one piece of land and neglect another. The sunshine is all-pervasive. Similarly, the warrior's discipline is not selective. The warrior never neglects his discipline or forgets it. His awareness and sensitivity are constantly extended. Even if a situation is very demanding or difficult, the warrior never gives up. He always conducts himself well, with gentleness and warmth, to begin with, and he always maintains his loyalty to sentient beings who are trapped in the setting-sun world. The warrior's duty is to generate warmth and compassion for others. He does this with complete absence of laziness. His discipline and dedication are unwavering.

When the warrior has unwavering discipline, he takes joy in the journey and joy in working with others. Rejoicing takes place throughout the warrior's life. Why are you always joyful? Because you have witnessed your basic goodness, because you have nothing to hang on to, and because you have experienced the sense of renunciation that we discussed earlier. Therefore, your mind and body are continually synchronized and always joyful. This joy is like music, which celebrates its own rhythm and melody. The celebration is continuous, in spite of the ups and downs of your personal life. That is what is meant by constantly being joyful.

Another aspect of the warrior's discipline is that it also contains discriminating awareness, or skillful intelligence. Therefore, it is like a bow and arrow. The arrow is sharp and penetrating; but to propel, or put into effect, that sharpness, you also need a bow. Similarly, the warrior is always inquisitive, interested in the world around him. But he also needs skillful action in order to apply his intelligence. When the arrow of intellect is joined with the bow of skillful means, then the warrior is never tempted by the seductions of the setting-sun world.

Temptation here refers to anything that promotes ego and goes against the vision of egolessness and basic goodness. There are many temptations, big and small. You can be tempted by a cookie or a million dollars. With the sharpness of the arrow, you can clearly see the setting sun, or any degraded activities that are going on—in yourself first, to be honest, and then in the rest of the world. But then to actually avoid temptation, you need the bow: you need to harness your insight with skillful action. This principle of the bow and arrow is learning to say "no" to ungenuineness, to say "no" to carelessness or crudeness, to say "no" to lack of wakefulness. In order to say "no" properly, you need both the bow and arrow. It has to be done with gentleness, which is the bow, and with sharpness, which is the arrow. Joining the two together, you realize that you *can* make a distinction; you can discriminate between indulging and appreciating. You can look at the world and see the way things actually work. Then you can overcome the myth, which is your own myth, that you can't say "no"—that you can't say "no" to the setting-sun world, or "no" to yourself when you feel like sinking into depression or indulgence. So the bow and arrow are connected first of all with overcoming the temptation of the setting-sun world.

When you learn to overcome temptation, then the arrow of intellect and the bow of action can manifest as trust in your world. This brings further inquisitiveness. You want to look into every situation and examine it, so that you won't be fooling yourself by relying on belief alone. Instead, you want to make a personal discovery of reality, through your own intelligence and ability. The sense of trust is that, when you apply your inquisitiveness, when you look into a situation, you know that you will get a definite response. If you take steps to accomplish something, that action will have a result—either failure or success. When you shoot your arrow, either it will hit the target or it will miss. Trust is knowing that there will be a message.

When you trust in those messages, the reflections of the phenomenal world, the world begins to seem like a bank, or reservoir, of richness. You feel that you are living in a rich world, one that never runs out of messages. A problem arises only if you try to manipulate a situation to your advantage or ignore it. Then you are violating your relationship of trust with the phenomenal world, so then the reservoir might dry up. But usually you will get a message first. If you are being too arrogant, you will find yourself being pushed down by heaven, and if you are being too timid, you will find yourself being raised up by earth.

Ordinarily, trusting in your world means that you expect to be taken care of or to be saved. You think that the world will give you what you want—or at least what you expect. But as a warrior, you are willing to take a chance; you are willing to expose yourself to the phenomenal world, and you trust that it will give you a message, either of success or failure. Those messages are regarded neither as punishment nor as congratulation. You trust, not in success, but in reality. You begin to realize that you usually fail when action and intellect are undisciplined or unsynchronized, and that you usually succeed when intelligence and action are fully joined. But whatever the result that comes from your action, that result is not an end in itself. You can always go beyond the result; it is the seed for a further journey. So a sense of continually going forward and celebrating your journey comes from practicing the warrior's discipline of the bow and arrow.

The final aspect of the warrior's discipline is meditative awareness. This principle of discipline is connected with how to take your seat in the warrior's world. The unwavering sun of discipline provides a path of exertion and joy that allows you to make your journey, while the bow and arrow principle provides a weapon to overcome temptation and penetrate the vast reservoir of resources in the phenomenal world. But neither of these can fulfill itself unless the warrior has a solid seat, or sense of presence, in his world. Meditative awareness enables the warrior to take his seat properly. It shows him how to regain his balance when he loses it, and how to use the messages of the phenomenal world to further his discipline, rather than simply being distracted or overwhelmed by the feedback.

The principle of meditative awareness can be likened to an echo that is always present in the warrior's world. The echo is experienced first in the sitting practice of meditation. When your thoughts wander in meditation or you become "lost in thought," the echo of your awareness reminds you to label your thoughts and return to the breath, return to a sense of being. Similarly. when the warrior starts to lose track of his discipline, by taking time off or indulging in a setting-sun mentality, his awareness is like an echo that bounces back on him.

At first, the echo may be fairly faint, but then it becomes louder and louder. The warrior is constantly reminded that he has to be on the spot, on the dot, because he is choosing to live in a world that does not give him the setting sun's concept of rest. Sometimes you might feel that the setting-sun world would be a tremendous relief. You don't have to work too hard there; you can flop and forget your echo. But then you may find it refreshing to return to the echo, because the setting-sun world is too deadly. There is not even an echo in that world.

From the echo of meditative awareness, you develop a sense of balance, which is a step towards taking command of your world. You feel that you are riding in the saddle, riding the fickle horse of mind. Even though the horse underneath you may move, you can still maintain your seat. As long as you have good posture in the saddle, you can overcome any startling or unexpected moves. And whenever you slip because you have a bad seat, you simply regain your posture; you don't fall off the horse. In the process of losing your awareness, you regain it *because* of the process of losing it.

Slipping, in itself, corrects itself. It happens automatically. You begin to feel highly skilled, highly trained.

The warrior's awareness is not based on the training of ultimate paranoia. It is based on the training of ultimate solidity—trusting in basic goodness. That does not mean that you have to be heavy or boring, but simply that you have a sense of being solidly rooted or established. You have trust and you have constant joyfulness; therefore you can't be startled. Sudden excitement or exaggerated reactions to situations need not occur at this level. You belong to the world of warriors. When little things happen—good or bad, right or wrong—you don't exaggerate them. You constantly come back to your saddle and your posture. The warrior is never amazed. If somebody comes up to you and says, "I'm going to kill you right now," or "I have a present of a million dollars for you," you are not amazed. You simply assume your seat in the saddle.

The principle of meditative awareness also gives you a good seat on this earth. When you take your seat on the earth properly, you do not need witnesses to confirm your validity. In a traditional story of the Buddha, when he attained enlightenment someone asked him, "How do we know that you are enlightened?" He said, "Earth is my witness." He touched the earth with his hand, which is known as the earth-touching *mudra*, or gesture. That is the same concept as holding your seat in the saddle. You are completely grounded in reality. Someone may say, "How do I know that you are not overreacting to situations?" You can say, simply, "My posture in the saddle speaks for itself."

At this point, you begin to experience the fundamental notion of fearlessness. You are willing to be awake in whatever situation may present itself to you, and you feel that you can take command of your life altogether, because you are not on the side of either success or failure. Success and failure are your journey. Of course, you may still experience fear within the context of fearlessness. There may be times on your journey when you are so petrified that you vibrate in the saddle, from your teeth to your hands to your legs. You are ardly sitting on the horse—you are practically levitating with fear. But even that is regarded as an expression of fearlessness, if you have a fundamental connection with the earth of your basic goodness.

TEN
LETTING GO

> *When you live your life in accordance with basic goodness, then you develop natural elegance. Your life can be spacious and relaxed, without having to be sloppy. You can actually let go of your depression and embarrassment about being a human being, and you can cheer up.*

THE RESULT of practicing the discipline of warriorship is that you learn to stop ambition and frivolity, and out of that, you develop a good sense of balance. Balance comes, not from holding on to a situation, but from making friends with heaven and earth. Earth is gravity, or practicality. Heaven is vision or the experience of open space in which you can uplift your posture, your head and shoulders. Balance comes from joining practicality with vision, or we could say, joining skill with spontaneity.

First, you must trust in yourself. Then you can also trust in the earth or gravity of a situation, and because of that, you can uplift yourself. At that point, your discipline becomes delightful rather than being an ordeal or a great demand. When you ride a horse, balance comes, not from freezing your legs to the saddle, but from learning to float with the movement of the horse as you ride. Each step is a dance, the rider's dance as well as the dance of the horse.

When discipline begins to be natural, a part of you, it is

54

very important to learn to let go. For the warrior, letting go is connected with relaxing within discipline, in order to experience freedom. Freedom here does not mean being wild or sloppy; rather it is letting yourself go so that you fully experience your existence as a human being. Letting go is completely conquering the idea that discipline is a punishment for a mistake or a bad deed that you have committed, or might like to commit. You have to completely conquer the feeling that there is something fundamentally wrong with your human nature and that therefore you need discipline to correct your behavior. As long as you feel that discipline comes from outside, there is still a lingering feeling that something is lacking in you. So letting go is connected with letting go of any vestiges of doubt or hesitation or embarrassment about being you as you are. You have to relax with yourself in order to fully realize that discipline is simply the expression of your basic goodness. You have to appreciate yourself, respect yourself, and let go of your doubt and embarrassment so that you can proclaim your goodness and basic sanity for the benefit of others.

In order to let go, first you have to train yourself in the discipline of renunciation as well as the aspects of discipline that were discussed in the last chapter. This is necessary so that you will not confuse letting go with aggression or arrogance. Without proper training, letting go can be confused with pushing yourself to the breaking point in order to prove to yourself that you are a brave and fearless person. This is too aggressive. Letting go also has nothing to do with enjoying yourself at other people's expense by promoting your own ego and "laying your trips" on others. Arrogance of that kind is not really based on letting go, in any case. It is based on a fundamental insecurity about yourself, which makes you insensitive rather than soft and gentle.

For example, a professional driver in an auto race can drive at two hundred miles an hour on the race track because of his training. He knows the limits of the engine and the steering and the tires; he knows the weight of the car, the road conditions, and the weather conditions. So he can drive fast without it becoming suicidal. Instead, it becomes a dance. But if you play with letting go before you have established a proper connection with discipline, then it is quite dangerous. If you are learning to ski and you try to let go and relax at an early level of your athletic training, you might easily fracture a bone. So if you mimic letting go, you may run into trouble.

You might think that, based on this discussion, you will never have sufficient training to let go and relax in your discipline. You might feel that you will never be ready to be a daring person. But once you have made a basic connection to discipline, it is time to let go of those doubts. If you are waiting for your discipline to become immaculate, that time will never come, unless you let go. When you begin to enjoy the discipline of warriorship, when it begins to feel natural, even though it may still feel very imperfect, that is the time to let go.

Obviously, letting go is more than just relaxation. It is relaxation based on being in tune with the environment, the world. One of the important principles of letting go is living in the challenge. But this does not mean living with a constant crisis. For example, suppose your banker calls and says that your account is overdrawn, and the same day your landlord tells you that you are about to be evicted for failing to pay your rent. To respond to this crisis, you get on the telephone and call all your friends to see if you can borrow enough money to avert the crisis. Living in the challenge is not based on responding to extraordinary demands that you have created for yourself by failing to relate to the details of your life. For the warrior, every moment is a challenge to be genuine, and each challenge is delightful. When you let go properly, you can relax and enjoy the challenge.

The setting-sun version of letting go is to take a vacation or to get drunk and become wild and sloppy and do outrageous things that, in your "right" mind, you would never contemplate. The Shambhala understanding is, obviously, quite different. For the warrior, letting go is not based on getting away from the constraints of ordinary life. It is quite the opposite. It is going further into your life, because you understand that your life, as it is, contains the means to unconditionally cheer you up and cure you of depression and doubt.

The setting-sun understanding of cheering up is talking

yourself into feeling better, rather than actually cheering up. When you wake up in the morning and get out of bed, you go into the bathroom and look at yourself in the mirror. Your hair is somewhat disheveled, you are half asleep, and there are bags under your eyes. In the setting-sun world, you say to yourself, with a big sigh, "Here we go again." You feel that you have to crank yourself up to get through the day. To use another example, when the Iranian revolutionaries were guarding the hostages at the American Embassy, they probably woke up in the morning with a feeling of delight: "Great! We have hostages next door!" That is a setting-sun version of cheerfulness.

Cheering up is not based on artificial willpower or creating an enemy and conquering him in order to make yourself feel more alive. Human beings have basic goodness, not next door, but *in* them already. When you look at yourself in the mirror, you can appreciate what you see, without worrying about whether what you see is what *should* be. You can pick up on the possibilities of basic goodness and cheer yourself up, if you just relax with yourself. Getting out of bed, walking into the bathroom, taking a shower, eating breakfast—you can appreciate whatever you do, without always worrying whether it fits your discipline or your plan for the day. You can have that much trust in yourself, and that will allow you to practice discipline much more thoroughly than if you constantly worry and try to check back to see how you are doing.

You can appreciate your life, even if it is an imperfect situation. Perhaps your apartment is run down and your furniture is old and inexpensive. You do not have to live in a palace. You can relax and let go wherever you are. Wherever you are, it *is* a palace. If you move into an apartment that was left in a mess, you can spend the time to clean it up, not because you feel bad or oppressed by dirt, but because you feel good. If you take the time to clean up and move in properly, you can transform a dumpy apartment into an accommodating home.

Human dignity is not based on monetary wealth. Affluent people may spend a great deal of money making their homes luxurious, but they may be creating artificial luxury. Dignity comes from using your inherent human resources, by doing things with your own bare hands—on the spot, properly and beautifully. You can do that: even in the worst of the worst situations, you can still make your life elegant.

Your body is an extension of basic goodness. It is the closest implement, or tool, that you have to express basic goodness, so appreciating your body is very important. The food you eat, the liquor you drink, the clothes you wear, and getting proper exercise are all important. You don't have to jog or do push-ups every day, but it is important to take an attitude of caring about your body. Even if you have a physical handicap, you don't have to feel that you are imprisoned by it. You can still respect your body and your life. Your dignity extends beyond your handicap. In the name of heaven and earth, you can afford to make love to yourself.

Shambhala vision is not purely a philosophy. It is actually training yourself to be a warrior. It is learning to treat yourself better, so that you can help to build an enlightened society. In that process, self-respect is very important and it is wonderful, absolutely excellent. You may not have money to buy expensive clothes, but you don't have to feel that your economic problems are driving you into the depression of the setting-sun world. You can still express dignity and goodness. You may be wearing jeans and a T-shirt, but you can be a dignified person wearing a T-shirt and cut-off jeans. The problem arises when you don't have respect for yourself and therefore for your clothes. If you go to bed in a depression and throw your clothes on the floor, that is a problem.

The basic point is that, when you live your life in accordance with basic goodness, then you develop natural elegance. Your life can be spacious and relaxed, without having to be sloppy. You can actually let go of your depression and embarrassment about being a human being, and you can cheer up. You don't have to blame the world for your problems. You can relax and appreciate the world.

Then there is a further stage of letting go, which is telling the truth. When you have doubts about yourself or doubts about the trustworthiness of your world, then you may feel that you have to manipulate the truth in order to protect yourself. For example, when you have a job interview, you may not be entirely truthful with your potential employer. You may feel that you have to bend the truth to get the job. You think that you have to make yourself appear better than you are. From the Shambhala point of view, honesty is the best policy. But telling the truth does not mean that you have to bare your innermost secrets and expose everything that you are ashamed of. You have nothing to be ashamed of! That is the basis for telling the truth. You may not be the greatest scholar or mechanic or artist or lover in the world, but what you are is genuinely, basically good. If you actually feel that, then you can let go of hesitation and self-consciousness and tell the truth, without exaggeration or denigration.

Then you begin to understand the importance of communicating openly with others. If you tell the truth to others, then they can also be open with you—maybe not immediately, but you are giving them the opportunity to express themselves honestly as well. When you do not say what you feel, you generate confusion for yourself and confusion for others. Avoiding the truth defeats the purpose of speech as communication.

Telling the truth is also connected with gentleness. A Shambhala person speaks gently: he or she doesn't bark. Gentle speech expresses your dignity, as does having good head and shoulders. It would be very strange if someone had good head and shoulders and began to bark. It would be very incongruous. Often when you talk to a person who doesn't know English, you find yourself yelling—as if you had to shout to be understood. That is exactly what should *not* happen. If you want to communicate with others, you don't have to shout and bang on the table in order to get them to listen. If you are telling the truth, then you can speak gently, and your words will have power.

The final stage of letting go is being without deception. Deception here does not refer to deliberately misleading others. Rather, your self-deception, your own hesitation and self-doubt, may confuse other people or actually deceive them. You may ask someone to help you make a decision: "Should I ask this person to marry me?" "Should I complain to so-and-so who was rude to me?" "Should I take this job?" "Should I go on vacation?" You are deceiving others if your question is not a genuine request for help but simply reflects your lack of self-confidence. Being without deception is actually a further extension of telling the truth: it is based on being truthful with yourself. When you have a sense of trusting in your own existence, then what you communicate to other people is genuine and trustworthy.

Self-deception often arises because you are afraid of your own intelligence and afraid that you won't be able to deal properly with your life. You are unable to acknowledge your own innate wisdom. Instead, you see wisdom as some monumental thing outside of yourself. That attitude has to be overcome. In order to be without deception, the only reference point you can rely on is the knowledge that basic goodness exists in you already. The certainty of that knowledge can be experienced in the practice of meditation. In meditation, you can experience a state of mind that is without second thoughts, free from fear and doubt. That unwavering state of mind is not swayed by the temporary ups and downs of thoughts and emotions. At first you may only have a glimpse. Through the practice of meditation, you glimpse a spark or a dot of unconditional, basic goodness. When you experience that dot, you may not feel totally free or totally good, but you realize that wakefulness, fundamental goodness, is there already. You can let go of hesitation, and therefore, you *can* be without deception. There is an uplifted quality to your life, which exists effortlessly. The result of letting go is contacting that uplifted energy, which allows you to completely join together discipline and delight, so that discipline becomes both effortless and splendid.

Everyone has experienced a wind of energy or power in their lives. For example, athletes feel a surge of energy when they are engaged in their sport. Or a person may experience a torrent of love or passion for another human being to whom he or she is attracted. Sometimes, we feel energy as a cool breeze of delight rather than a strong wind. For example, when you are hot and perspiring, if you take a shower, you feel so delightfully cool and energized at the same time.

Normally, we think that this energy comes from a definite source or has a particular cause. We associate it with the situation in which we became so energized. Athletes may become addicted to their sport because of the "rush" they experience. Some people become addicted to falling in love over and over again because they feel so good and alive when they are in love. The result of letting go is that you discover a bank of self-existing energy that is always available to you— beyond any circumstance. It actually comes from nowhere, but is always there. It is the energy of basic goodness.

This self-existing energy is called *windhorse* in the Shambhala teachings. The *wind* principle is that the energy of basic goodness is strong and exuberant and brilliant. It can actually radiate tremendous power in your life. But at the same time, basic goodness can be ridden, which is the principle of the *horse*. By following the disciplines of warriorship, particularly the discipline of letting go, you can harness the wind of goodness. In some sense the horse is never tamed— basic goodness never becomes your personal possession. But you can invoke and provoke the uplifted energy of basic goodness in your life. You begin to see how you can create basic goodness for yourself and others on the spot, fully and ideally, not only on a philosophical level, but on a concrete, physical level. When you contact the energy of windhorse, you can naturally let go of worrying about your own state of mind and you can begin to think of others. You feel a longing to share your discovery of goodness with your brothers and sisters, your mother and father, friends of all kinds who would also benefit from the message of basic goodness. So discovering windhorse is, first of all, acknowledging the strength of basic goodness in yourself and then fearlessly projecting that state of mind to others.

Experiencing the upliftedness of the world is a joyous situation, but it also brings sadness. It is like falling in love. When you are in love, being with your lover is both delightful and very painful. You feel both joy and sorrow. That is not a problem; in fact, it is wonderful. It is the ideal human emotion. The warrior who experiences windhorse feels the joy and sorrow of love in everything he does. He feels hot and cold, sweet and sour, simultaneously. Whether things go well or things go badly, whether there is success or failure, he feels sad and delighted at once.

In that way, the warrior begins to understand the meaning of unconditional confidence. The Tibetan word for confidence is *ziji*. *Zi* means "shine" or "glitter," and *ji* means "splendor," or "dignity," and sometimes also has the sense of "monolithic." So *ziji* expresses shining out, rejoicing while remaining dignified.

Sometimes confidence means that, being in a choiceless state, you trust in yourself and use your savings, information, strength, good memory, and stiff upper lip, and you accelerate your aggression and tell yourself that you're going to make it. That is the way of amateur warriors. In this case, confidence does not mean that you have confidence *in* something, but it is remaining in the state of confidence, free from competition or one-upmanship. This is an unconditional state in which you simply possess an unwavering state of mind that needs no reference point. There is no room for doubt; even the question of doubt does not occur. This kind of confidence contains gentleness, because the notion of fear does not arise; sturdiness, because in the state of confidence there is ever-present resourcefulness; and joy, because trusting in the heart brings a greater sense of humor. This confidence can manifest as majesty, elegance, and richness in a person's life. How to realize those qualities in your life is the topic of Part Two of this book.

༺༽ དོག་སྐྲག་ཅན་གྱི་སེམས་ཉིད་དེ། །རྒྱས་པའི་མཚོང་ར་དག་ཏུ་འཚུག
ཐག་ཏུ་ཐེ་ཚོམ་མེད་པ་ཡི། །ཆབ་ཅིང་གསལ་བའི་ནོ་མ་བསྐུན།
འཇིགས་པ་མེད་པའི་གྲིན་ཕས་ནི་ལ། །དགའ་ཞི་སྒོ་བའི་ཆུང་གསལ་གཡོན།
དེ་ལས་ན་ཚོད་ཀྲུས་པ་ན། །ཤིད་པའི་རྣོས་གར་སྐྱ་ཚིགས་ཀྱིས།
རང་བྱུང་རྗེ་དགོའི་ར་འབར་ཐྲེད། །དེ་ལས་ན་ཚོད་ཚེར་ཀྲུས་པ་ན།
གཏོད་མྱེ་གཞེ་འཇིད་སྒྱེལ་བའི་ཕྱིར། །དཔའ་བོའི་མདའ་ར་དག་ཏུ་ཞིད།
དེ་ལས་ན་ཚོད་ཚེར་ཀྲུས་པ་ས། །གཏོད་མྱེའི་རང་གཞེས་སད་པའི་ཕྱིར།
མཇེས་ཤིང་གཞི་འཇིད་སྐྱལ་པ་ཡི། །མེ་ཡེ་ཤིད་པར་བསྒུ་དུ་འཚུག
དོག་སྐྲག་ཅན་གྱི་སེམས་དེ་ཉིད། །དཔའ་བོའི་སེམས་སུ་འགྱུར་སྒྱིད་ཅིང་།
ཐག་ཏུ་གཞན་པའི་གརྗེ་འཇིད་དེ། །ཕྱོག་མཁན་མེད་པའི་མཁན་དུ་འཇལ།
                དེ་ཚོ་ཆར་ཆེར་ནི་མ་མཐོང་།།

That mind of fearfulness
Should be put in the cradle of loving-kindness
And suckled with the profound and brilliant milk
  of eternal doubtlessness.
In the cool shade of fearlessness,
Fan it with the fan of joy and happiness.
When it grows older,
With various displays of phenomena,
Lead it to the self-existing playground.
When it grows older still,
To awaken primordial self-nature,
Let it see the society of men
Which possesses beauty and dignity.
Then the fearful mind
Can change into the warrior's mind,
And that eternally youthful confidence
Can expand into space without beginning or end.
At that point it sees the Great Eastern Sun.

PART TWO

SACREDNESS:
THE WARRIOR'S WORLD

ELEVEN
NOWNESS

We need to find the link between our traditions and our present experience of life. Nowness, or the magic of the present moment, is what joins the wisdom of the past with the present.

FROM THE MOMENT YOU ARE BORN, when you first cry and breathe free from your mother's womb, you are a separate individual. Of course, there is still emotional attachment, or an emotional umbilical cord, that connects you to your parents, but as you grow older and pass from infancy into youth and maturity, as each year passes, your attachment decreases. You become an individual who can function separate from your mother and father.

In that journey through life, human beings must overcome the neurotic attachment of being the child-of-somebody. The principles of warriorship that we discussed in Part One are connected with how individuals can develop personal discipline so that they become mature and independent and therefore experience a sense of personal freedom. But then, once that development has taken place, it is equally important to share the comradeship of human society. This is an organic expression of the greater vision of warriorship. It is based on the appreciation of a larger world. In the process of

67

becoming a warrior, you naturally begin to feel a deep fellow-ship with human beings. That is the real basis for helping others and, ultimately, for making a genuine contribution to society.

However, your connection to other human beings and your concern for their welfare have to be manifested person-ally, practically. Abstractly caring about others is not enough. The most practical and immediate way to begin sharing with others and working for their benefit is to work with your own domestic situation and to expand from there. So an important step in becoming a warrior is to become a family person, someone who respects his or her everyday domestic life and is committed to uplifting that situation.

You can't help society purely on the basis of your vision for the nation or the world. There are many ideas of how to organize a society so that it will fulfill people's needs. There is, of course, the popular idea of democratic rule, rule by the people. Another approach is that rule by an elite will produce a progressive society. A third idea is to take a scientific approach to ruling, in which natural resources are equally distributed and a completely balanced ecology is created. These and other ideas may have value, but they must be integrated with an individual human being's experience of domestic life. Otherwise you have a huge gap between your grand vision for society and the reality of everyday existence. To use one model of family life: a man and a woman meet, they fall in love and marry, they set up a household and then they may have children. Then they have to worry about whether the dishwasher is working or whether they have the money to buy a new stove. As the children grow up, they go to school to learn to read and write. Some children may have an ideal relationship with their parents, but the family has money problems. Or there may be lots of money but a very difficult family relationship. We go back and forth between those problems. We should respect life on that mundane level, because the only way to implement our vision for society is to bring it down to the situation of a single household.

Becoming a family person also means taking pride in the wisdom of your family heritage. From the Shambhala point of view, respecting your family and your upbringing has nothing to do with separating yourself from others or becoming arrogant about your ancestry. Rather, it is based on realizing that the structure and experience of family life actually reflect the deep-seated wisdom of a culture. That wisdom has been passed down to you, and it is actually present in your everyday, domestic life. So by appreciating your family tradition, you are opening yourself further to the richness of the world.

I remember very clearly the experience of discovering my own connection to family heritage. I was born in a cowshed in Eastern Tibet, where people have never seen a tree. The people of that region live on pasture land that has no trees or even bushes. They subsist on meat and milk products throughout the whole year. I was born a son of this genuine earth, the son of a peasant. At a very early age I was recognized as a *tulku,* or incarnate lama, and I was taken to the Surmang monasteries to receive my training and become a monk. So, almost from birth, I was taken out of my family situation and placed in a monastic environment. I was always called by my religious name, Trungpa Rinpoche. Nevertheless, I never forgot my birth.

When I moved to the monastery, my mother accompanied me and stayed with me for several years, until I was old enough to begin my formal education. Once when I was about four or five I asked my mother: "Mother, what is our name?" She was very shy. She said, "What do you mean by *our*? You know that your name is Trungpa Rinpoche." But I insisted. I asked, "What is our name? Our family name? Where do we come from?" And she said, "Well, you should forget that. It's a very humble name, and you might be ashamed of it." But I still insisted, saying, "What is our family name? What is it?"

At the time I was playing with some pickled radishes that are fed to horses. I was picking up these little pickled radishes off the floor outside the monastery kitchen. Tulkus are not supposed to eat them, but I was chewing on one, and I kept saying, "Mother, what is our name? What is our family name?" I was about to bite into another pickled radish, which was dirty, and she was very concerned, and she was so shy. But she was also intrigued that I had asked. We had an intense moment of relating with each other.

I remember that it was a sunny day, and the sun shone from a window in the roof onto her face. She looked old and young at the same time. I kept asking, "What is our family name?" And finally she said, "Mukpo, Mukpo of course. But don't bite that pickle! It's for the horses." I'm afraid I did bite it, and I remember chewing it. It was very crunchy and tasted something like a *tsukemono*, a kind of Japanese pickle, and I liked it very much. I looked at my mother and asked, "Does that mean I'm Mukpo too?" She wasn't quite sure. She said, "Well, you are Rinpoche!" Then I distinctly remember asking her whether I was her son who came out of her body, and at first she said, "Yes." But then she said, "Well, maybe I'm an inhuman being, a subhuman being. I have a woman's body; I had an inferior birth. Please go back to your quarters." And she took me in her arms and carried me from the kitchen annex to my quarters. Nonetheless, I have kept the name Mukpo as my family name, my identity and pride.

My mother was a very gentle person. As far as I know, she never did anything aggressive, and she was always accommodating and kind to others. I learned a great deal about the principles of human society from the wisdom of my mother.

In modern times, the emphasis has shifted away from the family as the focus of society. Earlier, the focus on the family was partly a matter of survival. For example, before there were hospitals and doctors, a woman often relied on her mother to help her deliver her children and for help in raising the children. But now, medical research has incorporated the grandmothers' wisdom, and children are delivered by doctors in a hospital maternity ward. In most areas, the grandparents' wisdom is no longer needed, and they have no role to play. They end up in an old age home or a retirement community, and occasionally they come to visit their grandchildren and watch how nicely they play.

In some societies, people used to set up shrines to venerate their ancestors. Even today, in such a modern society as Japan, there is still a strong tradition of ancestor worship. You may think that such practices are purely a function of primitive thinking or superstition, but in fact, the veneration of your ancestral lineage can be a sign of respect for the accumulated wisdom of your culture. I am not suggesting that we reinstate ancestor worship, but it is necessary to appreciate that, for many thousands of years, human beings have been collecting wisdom. We should appreciate the accomplishments of our ancestors: that human beings learned to make tools, that they developed knives and bows and arrows, that they learned to cut down trees, to cook their food and to add spices to it. We should not ignore the contributions of the past.

How to construct a building has thousands of years of history behind it. First human beings lived in caves; then they learned how to build huts. Then they learned how to construct a building with pillars and columns. Finally they learned how to construct a building without columns in the center, with arches spanning the ceiling, which is a remarkable discovery. Such wisdom has to be respected. It is not regarded as a setting-sun approach at all. Many people must have been crushed when they tried to build a structure without central columns and it collapsed. People must have sacrificed their lives until a model was developed that worked. You might say such an accomplishment is insignificant, but on the other hand, the failure to appreciate the resourcefulness of human existence—which we call basic goodness—has become one of the world's biggest problems.

However, venerating the past in itself will not solve the world's problems. We need to find the link between our traditions and our present experience of life. *Nowness*, or the magic of the present moment, is what joins the wisdom of the past with the present. When you appreciate a painting or a piece of music or a work of literature, no matter when it was created, you appreciate it *now*. You experience the same nowness in which it was created. It is always *now*.

The way to experience nowness is to realize that this very moment, this very point in your life, is always *the* occasion. So the consideration of where you are and what you are, on the spot, is very important. That is one reason that your family situation, your domestic everyday life, is so important. You should regard your home as sacred, as a golden opportunity to experience nowness. Appreciating sacredness begins very simply by taking an interest in all the details of your life. Interest is simply applying awareness to what goes on in your everyday life—awareness while you're cooking, awareness while you're driving, awareness while you're changing diapers, even awareness while you're arguing. Such awareness can help to free you from speed, chaos, neurosis, and resentment of all kinds. It can free you from the obstacles to nowness, so that you can cheer up on the spot, all the time.

The principle of nowness is also very important to any effort to establish an enlightened society. You may wonder what the best approach is to helping society and how you can know that what you are doing is authentic or good. The only answer is nowness. *Now* is the important point. That *now* is a real *now*. If you are unable to experience *now*, then you are corrupted because you are looking for another *now*, which is impossible. If you do that, there can only be past or future.

When corruption enters a culture, it is because that culture ceases to be *now;* it becomes past and future. Periods in history when great art was created, when learning advanced, or peace spread, were all *now*. Those situations happened at the very moment of their *now*. But after *now* happened, then those cultures lost their *now*.

You have to maintain nowness, so that you don't duplicate corruption, so that you don't corrupt *now*, and so that you don't have false synonyms for *now* at all. The vision of enlightened society is that tradition and culture and wisdom and dignity can be experienced *now* and kept *now* on everyone's part. In that way there can never be corruption of any kind at all.

Enlightened society must rest on a good foundation. The nowness of your family situation is that foundation. From it, you can expand. By regarding your home as sacred, you can enter into domestic situations with awareness and with delight, rather than feeling that you are subjecting yourself to chaos. It may seem that washing dishes and cooking dinner are completely mundane activities, but if you apply awareness in any situation, then you are training your whole being so that you will be able to open yourself further, rather than narrowing your existence.

You may feel that you have a good vision for society but that your life is filled with hassles—money problems, problems relating to your spouse or caring for your children—and that those two things, vision and ordinary life, are opposing one another. But vision and practicality *can* be joined together in nowness.

Too often people think that solving the world's problems is based on conquering the earth, rather than on touching the earth, touching ground. That is one definition of the setting-sun mentality: trying to conquer the earth so that you can ward off reality. There are all kinds of deodorant sprays to keep you from smelling the real world, and all kinds of processed food to keep you from tasting raw ingredients. Shambhala vision is not trying to create a fantasy world where no one has to see blood or experience a nightmare. Shambhala vision is based on living on this earth, the real earth, the earth that grows crops, the earth that nurtures your existence. You can learn to live on this earth: how to camp, how to pitch a tent, how to ride a horse, milk a cow, build a fire. Even though you may be living in a city in the twentieth century, you can learn to experience the sacredness, the *nowness*, of reality. That is the basis for creating an enlightened society.

TWELVE
DISCOVERING MAGIC

Any perception can connect us to reality properly and fully. What we see doesn't have to be pretty, particularly; we can appreciate anything that exists. There is some principle of magic in everything, some living quality. Something living, something real, is taking place in everything.

IN TWENTIETH-CENTURY SOCIETY, the appreciation of simplicity has almost been lost. From London to Tokyo, there are problems with trying to create pleasure and comfort out of speed. The world is mechanized to such an extent that you don't even have to think. You just push a button and a computer gives you the answer. You don't have to learn to count. You press a button, and a machine counts for you. Casualness has become increasingly popular, because people think in terms of efficiency rather than appreciation. Why bother to wear a tie, if the purpose of wearing clothes is just to cover your body? If the reason for eating food is only to fill your stomach and provide nutrition, why bother to look for the best meat, the best butter, the best vegetables?

But the reality of the world is something more than the life style that the twentieth-century world has embraced. Pleasure has been cheapened, joy has been reduced, happiness has been computerized. The goal of warriorship is to reconnect to the nowness of reality, so that you can go forward without destroying simplicity, without destroying your connection to this earth. In the last chapter, we discussed the importance of nowness as a way of joining together the wisdom of the past with the challenge of the present. In this chapter, we are going to discuss how to discover the ground of nowness. In order to rediscover nowness, you have to look back, back to where you came from, back to the original state. In this case, looking back is not looking back in time, going back several thousand years. It is looking back into your own mind, to before history began, before thinking began, before thought ever occurred. When you are in contact with this original ground, then you are never confused by the illusions of past and future. You are able to rest continuously in nowness.

This original state of being can be likened to a primordial, or cosmic, mirror. By *primordial* we mean unconditioned, not caused by any circumstances. Something primordial is not a reaction for or against any situation. All conditionality comes from unconditionality. Anything that is made has to come from what was unmade, to begin with. If something is conditioned, it has been created or formed. In the English language, we speak of formulating ideas or plans, or we may say, "How should we *form* our organization?" or we may talk about the formation of a cloud. In contrast to that, the unconditioned is free from being formed, free from creation. This unconditioned state is likened to a primordial *mirror* because, like a mirror, it is willing to reflect anything, from the gross level up to the refined level, and it still remains as it is. The basic frame of reference of the cosmic mirror is quite vast, and it is free from any bias: kill or cure, hope or fear.

The way to look back and experience the state of being of the cosmic mirror is simply to relax. In this case relaxation is quite different from the setting-sun idea of flopping or taking time off, entertaining yourself with a good vacation. Relaxation here refers to relaxing the mind, letting go of the anxiety and concepts and depression that normally bind you. The way to relax, or rest the mind in nowness, is through the practice of meditation. In Part One, we discussed how the practice of meditation is connected to renouncing small-mindedness and personal territory. In meditation you are neither "for" nor "against" your experience. That is, you don't praise some thoughts and condemn others, but you take an unbiased approach. You let things be as they are, without judgment, and in that way you yourself learn to be, to express your existence directly, nonconceptually. That is the ideal state of relaxation, which allows you to experience the nowness of the cosmic mirror. In fact, it is *already* the experience of the cosmic mirror.

If you are able to relax—relax to a cloud by looking at it, relax to a drop of rain and experience its genuineness—you can see the unconditionality of reality, which remains very simply in things as they are, very simply. When you are able to look at things without saying, "This is for me or against me," "I can go along with this," or "I cannot go along with this," then you are experiencing the state of being of the cosmic mirror, the wisdom of the cosmic mirror. You may see a fly buzzing; you may see a snowflake; you may see ripples of water; you may see a black widow spider. You may see anything, but you can actually look at all of those things with simple and ordinary, but appreciative, perception.

You experience a vast realm of perceptions unfolding. There is unlimited sound, unlimited sight, unlimited taste, unlimited feeling and so on. The realm of perception is limitless, so limitless that perception itself is primordial, unthinkable, beyond thought. There are so many perceptions that they are beyond imagination. There are a vast number of sounds. There are sounds that you have never heard. There are sights and colors that you have never seen. There are feelings that you have never experienced before. There are endless fields of perception.

Perception here is not just what you perceive but the whole act of perceiving—the interaction between consciousness, the sense organs and the sense fields, or the objects of perception. In some religious traditions, sense perceptions are regarded as problematic, because they arouse worldly desires. However, in the Shambhala tradition, which is a secular tradition rather than a religious one, sense perceptions are regarded as sacred. They are regarded as basically good. They are a natural gift, a natural ability that human beings have. They are a source of wisdom. If you don't see sights, if you don't hear sounds, if you don't taste food, you have no way to communicate with the phenomenal world at all. But because of the extraordinary vastness of perception, you have possibilities of communicating with the depth of the world—the world of sight, the world of sound—the greater world.

In other words, your sense faculties give you access to possibilities of deeper perception. Beyond ordinary perception, there is super-sound, super-smell and super-feeling existing in your state of being. These can be experienced only by training yourself in the depth of meditation practice, which clarifies any confusion or cloudiness and brings out the precision, sharpness, and wisdom of perception—the nowness of your world. In meditation, you experience the precision of breath going in and out. You feel your breath: it is *so* good. You breathe out, breath dissolves: it is so sharp and good, it is so extraordinary that ordinary preoccupations become superfluous. So meditation practice brings out the supernatural, if I may use that word. You do not see ghosts or become telepathic, but your perceptions become super-natural, simply super-natural.

Normally, we limit the meaning of perceptions. Food reminds us of eating; dirt reminds us to clean the house; snow reminds us that we have to clean off the car to get to work; a face reminds us of our love or hate. In other words, we fit what we see into a comfortable or familiar scheme. We shut any vastness or possibilities of deeper perception out of our hearts by fixating on our own interpretation of phenomena. But it is possible to go beyond personal interpretation, to let vastness into our hearts through the medium of perception. We always have a choice: we can limit our perception so that we close off vastness, or we can allow vastness to touch us.

When we draw down the power and depth of vastness into a single perception, then we are discovering and invoking magic. By magic we do not mean unnatural power over the phenomenal world, but rather the discovery of innate or primordial wisdom in the world as it is. The wisdom we are discovering is wisdom without beginning, something naturally wise, the wisdom of the cosmic mirror. In Tibetan, this magical quality of existence, or natural wisdom, is called *drala*. *Dra* means "enemy" or "opponent" and *la* means "above." So *drala* literally means "above the enemy," "beyond the enemy." *Drala* is the unconditioned wisdom and power of the world that are beyond any dualism; therefore drala is above any enemy or conflict. It is wisdom beyond aggression. It is the self-existing wisdom and power of the cosmic mirror that are reflected both in us and in our world of perception.

One of the key points in discovering drala principle is realizing that your own wisdom as a human being is not separate from the power of things as they are. They are both reflections of the unconditioned wisdom of the cosmic mirror. Therefore there is no fundamental separation or duality between you and your world. When you can experience those two things together, as one, so to speak, then you have access to tremendous vision and power in the world—you find that they are inherently connected to your own vision, your own being. That is discovering magic. We are not talking here about an intellectual revelation; we are speaking of actual experience. We are talking about how we actually perceive reality. The discovery of drala may come as an extraordinary smell, a fantastic sound, a vivid color, an unusual taste. Any perception can connect us to reality properly and fully. What we see doesn't have to be pretty, particularly; we can appreciate anything that exists. There is some principle of magic in everything, some living quality. Something living, something real is taking place in everything.

When we see things as they are, they make sense to us: the way leaves move when they are blown by the wind, the way rocks get wet when there are snowflakes sitting on them. We see how things display their harmony and their chaos at the same time. So we are never limited by beauty alone, but we appreciate all sides of reality properly.

Many stories and poems written for children describe the experience of invoking the magic of a simple perception. One example is "Waiting at the Window" from *Now We Are Six*, by A. A. Milne. It is a poem about spending several hours on a rainy day looking out the window, watching drops of water come down and make patterns on the glass. Reading this poem, you see the window, the rainy day, and the child with his face pressed to the glass watching the raindrops, and you feel the child's sense of delight and wonder. The poems of Robert Louis Stevenson in *A Child's Garden of Verses* have a similar quality of using very ordinary experiences to communicate the depth of perception. The poems "My Shadow," "My Kingdom," and "Armies in the Fire" exemplify this. The fundamental vastness of the world cannot be expressed directly in words, but in children's literature, very often it is possible to express that vastness in simplicity.

The Little Prince by Antoine de Saint Exupéry is another wonderful example of literature that evokes the sense of ordinary, or elemental, magic. At one point in this story, the little prince meets a fox. The prince is very lonely and wants the fox to play with him, but the fox says that he cannot play unless he is tamed. The little prince asks the meaning of the word "tame." The fox explains that it means "to establish ties" in such a way that the fox will become unique to the little prince, and the prince unique to the fox. Later, after the fox has been tamed and the little prince must leave him, the fox also tells the prince what he calls "my secret, a very simple secret," which is, "it is only with the heart that one can see rightly; what is essential is invisible to the eye."

Saint Exupéry has a different vocabulary here for describing the discovery of magic, or drala, but the experience is basically the same. Discovering drala is indeed to establish ties to your world, so that each perception becomes unique. It is to see with the heart, so that what is invisible to the eye becomes visible as the living magic of reality. There may be thousands or billions of perceptions, but they are still one. If you see one candle, you know exactly what all the candles in the whole world look like. They are all made out of fire, flame. Seeing one drop of water can be seeing all water.

Drala could almost be called an entity. It is not quite on the level of a god or gods, but it is an individual strength that does exist. Therefore, we not only speak of drala principle, but we speak of meeting the "dralas." The dralas are the elements of reality—water of water, fire of fire, earth of earth—anything that connects you with the elemental quality of reality, anything that reminds you of the depth of perception. There are dralas in the rocks or the trees or the mountains or a snowflake or a clod of dirt. Whatever is there, whatever you come across in your life, those are the dralas of reality. When you make that connection with the elemental quality of the world, you are meeting dralas on the spot; at that point, you are meeting them. That is the basic existence of which all human beings are capable. We always have possibilities of discovering magic. Whether it is medieval times or the twentieth century, the possibility of magic is always there.

A particular example of meeting drala, in my personal experience, is flower arranging. Whatever branches you find, none of them is rejected as ugly. They can always be included. You have to learn to see their place in the situation; that is the key point. So you never reject anything. That is how to make a connection with the dralas of reality.

Drala energy is like the sun. If you look in the sky, the sun is there. By looking at it, you don't produce a new sun. You may feel that you created or made today's sun by looking at it, but the sun is eternally there. When you discover the sun in the sky, you begin to communicate with it. Your eyes begin to relate with the light of the sun. In the same way, drala principle is always there. Whether you care to communicate with it or not, the magical strength and wisdom of reality are always there. That wisdom abides in the cosmic mirror. By relaxing the mind, you can reconnect with that primordial, original ground, which is completely pure and simple. Out of that, through the medium of your perceptions, you can discover magic, or drala. You actually can connect your own intrinsic wisdom with a sense of greater wisdom or vision beyond you.

You might think that something extraordinary will happen to you when you discover magic. Something extra-ordinary does happen. You simply find yourself in the realm of utter reality, complete and thorough reality.

THIRTEEN

HOW TO INVOKE MAGIC

> *When you express gentleness and precision in your environment, then real brilliance and power can descend onto that situation. If you try to manufacture that presence out of your own ego, it will never happen. You cannot own the power and the magic of this world. It is always available, but it does not belong to anyone.*

THE PHENOMENAL WORLD that all human beings experience is fickle and flexible and also merciless. You often wonder whether you can ride on that fickle and merciless situation or whether it is going to ride on you. To use an analogy, either you are riding on a donkey or the donkey is riding on you. Ordinarily, in your experience of the world it is questionable who is riding on whom. The more you struggle to gain the upper hand, the more speed and aggression you manufacture to overcome your obstacles, the more you become subject to the phenomenal world. The real challenge is to transcend that duality altogether. It is possible to contact energy that is beyond dualism, beyond aggression—energy that is neither for you nor against you. That is the energy of drala.

Drala is not a god or spirit, but fundamentally it is connecting the wisdom of your own being with the power of things as they are. If you are able to connect those two things, out of that, you can discover magic in everything. But there is still a question as to what it is that allows you to make that connection. In the last chapter, the drala principle was likened to the sun. Although the sun is always in the sky, what is it that causes you to look up and see that it is there? Although magic is always available, what allows you to discover it? The basic definition of drala is "energy beyond aggression." The only way to contact that energy is to experience a gentle state of being in yourself. So the discovery of drala is not coincidental. To connect with the fundamental magic of reality, there has to be gentleness and openness in you already. Otherwise, there is no way to recognize the energy of nonaggression, the energy of drala, in the world. So the individual training and discipline of the Shambhala warrior are the necessary foundation for experiencing drala.

The setting-sun world, based on fear of oneself and fear of death, has no connection to drala principle. The cowardice and aggression of the setting-sun outlook actually dispel any magical possibilities, any possibilities of experiencing the genuine and brilliant qualities of reality. The opposite of setting-sun outlook and the way to invoke drala is to manifest the vision of the Great Eastern Sun. Great Eastern Sun vision, which we discussed in earlier chapters, is the expression of true human goodness, based not on arrogance or aggression, but on gentleness and openness. It is the way of the warrior.

The essence of this way or path is transcending cowardice and manifesting bravery. That is the best and only way to invoke drala: by creating an atmosphere of bravery. We have already talked in earlier chapters about the qualities of bravery. The fundamental aspect of bravery is *being without deception*. Deception in this case is self-deception, doubting yourself so that you are cut off from the vision of the Great Eastern Sun. The dralas can only descend onto your existence when you have properly prepared the ground. If there is the slightest deception, you will dispel drala. From that point of view, deception is the magic of the setting sun.

Usually if we say someone is brave, we mean that he is not afraid of any enemy or he is willing to die for a cause or he is never intimidated. The Shambhala understanding of bravery is quite different. Here bravery is the courage to be—to live in the world without any deception and with tremendous kindness and caring for others. You might wonder how this can bring magic into your life. The ordinary idea of magic is that you can conquer the elements, so that you can turn earth into fire or fire into water or ignore the law of gravity and fly. But true magic is the magic of *reality*, as it is: the earth of earth, the water of water—communicating with the elements so that, in some sense, they become one with you. When you develop bravery, you make a connection with the elemental quality of existence. Bravery begins to heighten your existence, that is, to bring out the brilliant and genuine qualities of your environment and of your own being. So you begin to contact the magic of reality—which is already there in some sense. You actually can attract the power and strength and the primordial wisdom that arise from the cosmic mirror.

At that point, you begin to see how you can influence your environment so that the drala principle is reflected in every activity of your life. You see that you can actually organize your life in such a way that you magnetize magic, or drala, to manifest brilliance and elegance in your world. The way to do this is divided into three parts, which are called the three ways to invoke drala.

The first is invoking *external drala*, which is invoking magic in your physical environment. This may be as small and limited as a one-room apartment or as large as a mansion or a hotel. How you organize and care for that space is very important. If it is chaotic and messy, then no drala will enter into that environment. On the other hand, we are not talking about taking a course in interior decoration and spending a great deal of money on furniture and rugs to create a "model environment." For the warrior, invoking external drala is creating harmony in your environment in order to encourage awareness and attention to detail. In that way, your physical environment promotes your discipline of warriorship. Beyond that, how you organize your physical space should be based on concern for others, sharing your world by creating an accommodating environment. The point is not to make a self-conscious statement about yourself, but to make your world available to others. When that begins to happen, then it is possible that something else will come along as well. That is, when you express gentleness and precision in your environment, then real brilliance and power can descend onto that situation. If you try to manufacture that presence out of your own ego, it will never happen. You cannot own the power and the magic of this world. It is always available, but it does not belong to anyone.

There are many other examples of invoking external drala. I have read, for instance, that some American Indians in the Southwest grow vegetables in the desert sands. The soil, from an objective standpoint, is completely infertile. If you just threw a handful of seeds into that earth, nothing would grow. But the Indians have been cultivating that soil for generations; they have a deep connection to that earth and they care for it. To them it is sacred ground, and because of that their plants grow. That is real magic. The attitude of sacredness towards your environment will bring drala. You may live in a dirt hut with no floor and only one window, but if you regard that space as sacred, if you care for it with your heart and mind, then it will be a palace.

The idea of sacred space is also what gives grandeur to a great cathedral, like Chartres, or to a house of government, like the English Houses of Parliament. Churches are consciously built as sacred places, whereas a house of government may never have been conceived of as "sacred" by its architects. Nevertheless, those places have a presence that is more than the structure of the building or the beauty of the materials used to construct them. They radiate a particular atmosphere that you cannot help but feel.

The Greeks and the Romans laid out their cities with some understanding of external drala. You might say that putting a fountain in the center of a square or at a crossroads is a random choice. But when you come upon that fountain, it does not feel random at all. It is in its own proper place and it seems to enhance the space around it. In modern times, we don't think very highly of the Romans, with all of their debauchery and corrupt rulers. We tend to downplay the wisdom of their culture. Certainly, corruption dispels drala. But there was some power and wisdom in the Roman civilization, which we should not overlook.

In summary, invoking the external drala principle is connected with organizing your environment so that it becomes a sacred space. This begins with the organization of your personal, household environment, and beyond that, it can include much larger environments, such as a city or even an entire country.

Then, there is invoking *internal drala*, which is how to invoke drala in your body. Basically, the experience of internal drala is that you feel oneness in your body—oneness in the sense that your head, your shoulders, your torso, your arms, your genitals, your knees, your legs, and your toes all hang together as one basically good human body. You feel no quarrel between your head and shoulders, between your toes and legs, and so forth. It doesn't really matter whether your hair is growing grey or you are developing wrinkles on your face or your hands are shaky. There is still a feeling that your body has its own fitness, its own unity. When you look, you hear; when you hear, you smell; when you smell, you taste; when you taste, you feel. All of your sense perceptions work as one unit, as one basic goodness, one expression of basic health.

You invoke internal drala through your relationship to your personal habits, how you handle the details of dressing, eating, drinking, sleeping. We could use clothing as an example. For the warrior, clothing actually provides an armor of discipline, which wards off attacks from the setting-sun world. It is not that you hide behind your clothes because you are afraid to manifest yourself as a good warrior, but rather that, when you wear good, well-fit clothes, your clothing can both ward off casualness and invite tremendous dignity.

Sometimes if your clothes fit you well, you feel that they are too tight. If you dress up, you may feel constricted by wearing a necktie or a suit or a tight fitting skirt or dress. The idea of invoking internal drala is not to give in to the allure of casualness. The occasional irritation coming from your neck, the crotch of your pants, or your waist is usually a good sign. It means that your clothes fit you well, but your neurosis doesn't fit your clothes. The modern approach is often free and casual. That is the attraction of polyester leisure suits. You feel stiff if you are dressed up. You are tempted to take off your tie or your jacket or your shoes. Then you can hang out and put your feet on the table and act freely, hoping that your mind will act freely at the same time. But at that point your mind begins to dribble. It begins to leak, and garbage of all kinds comes out of your mind. That version of relaxation does not provide real freedom at all. Therefore, for the warrior, wearing well-fit clothing is regarded as wearing a suit of armor. How you dress can actually invoke upliftedness and grace.

Internal drala also comes out of making a proper relationship to food, by taking an interest in your diet. This does not necessarily mean that you should shop around for the best gourmet items. But you can take the time to plan good, nutritious meals, and you can enjoy cooking your food, eating it, and then cleaning up and putting the leftovers away. Beyond that, you invoke internal drala by developing greater awareness of how you use your mouth altogether. You put food in your mouth; you drink liquids through your mouth; you smoke cigarettes in your mouth. It is as if the mouth were a big hole or a big garbage pail: you put everything through it. Your mouth is the biggest gate: you talk out of it, you cry out of it, and you kiss out of it. You use your mouth so much that it becomes a sort of cosmic gateway. Imagine that you were being watched by Martians. They would be amazed by how much you use your mouth.

To invoke internal drala you have to pay attention to how you use your mouth. Maybe you don't need to use it as much as you think. Appreciating your world doesn't mean that you must consume everything you see all the time. When you eat, you can eat slowly and moderately, and you can appreciate what you eat. When you talk, it isn't necessary to continually blurt out everything that is on your mind. You can say what you have to say, gently, and then you can stop. You can let someone else talk, or you can appreciate the silence.

The basic idea of invoking internal drala is that you can synchronize, or harmonize, your body and your connection to the phenomenal world. This synchronization, or connectedness, is something that you can actually see. You can see people's connection to internal drala by the way they behave: the way they pick up their teacups, the way they smoke their cigarettes, or the way they run their hands through their hair. Whatever you do always manifests how you are feeling about yourself and your environment—whether you feel kindness towards yourself or resentment and anger towards yourself; whether you feel good about your environment or whether you feel bad about your environment. That can always be detected by your gait and your gestures—always. It is as if you were married to your phenomenal world. All the little details—the way you turn on the tap before you take a shower, the way you brush your teeth—reflect your connection or disconnection with the world. When that connection is completely synchronized, then you are experiencing internal drala.

Finally, there is what is known as invoking *secret drala*, which is the product of invoking the external and internal drala principles. Because you have created a sacred environment around you and because you have synchronized your body so beautifully, so immaculately, therefore you provoke tremendous wakefulness, tremendous nowness in your state of mind.

The chapter on "Letting Go" introduced the idea of windhorse, or riding on the energy of basic goodness in your life. Windhorse is a translation of the Tibetan *lungta*. *Lung* means "wind" and *ta* means "horse." Invoking secret drala is the experience of raising windhorse, raising a wind of delight and power and riding on, or conquering, that energy. Such wind can come with great force, like a typhoon that can blow down trees and buildings and create huge waves in the water. The personal experience of this wind comes as a feeling of being completely and powerfully in the present. The *horse* aspect is that, in spite of the power of this great wind, you also feel stability. You are never swayed by the confusion of life, never swayed by excitement or depression. You can ride on the energy of your life. So windhorse is not purely movement and speed, but it includes practicality and discrimination, a natural sense of skill. This quality of lungta is like the four legs of a horse, which make it stable and balanced. Of course, in this case you are not riding an ordinary horse; you are riding a windhorse.

By invoking the external and internal drala principles, you raise a wind of energy and delight in your life. You begin to feel natural power and upliftedness manifesting in your existence. Then, having raised your windhorse, you can accommodate whatever arises in your state of mind. There is no problem or hesitation of any kind. So the fruition of invoking secret drala is that, having raised windhorse, you experience a state of mind that is free from subconscious gossip, free from hesitation and disbelief. You experience the very moment of your state of mind. It is fresh and youthful and virginal. That very moment is innocent and genuine. It does not contain doubt or disbelief at all. It is gullible, in the positive sense, and it is completely fresh. Secret drala is experiencing that very moment of your state of mind, which is the essence of nowness. You actually experience being able to connect yourself to the inconceivable vision and wisdom of the cosmic mirror on the spot. At the same time, you realize that this experience of nowness can join together the vastness of primordial wisdom with both the wisdom of past traditions and the realities of contemporary life. So in that way, you begin to see how the warrior's world of sacredness can be created altogether. In the following chapters, we will investigate that world more thoroughly.

OVERCOMING ARROGANCE

*When you are fully gentle, without arrogance and
without aggression, you see the brilliance of the
universe. You develop a true perception of the
universe.*

IN THE LAST CHAPTER we discussed ways to invoke the drala
principle. In this and the next chapter we are going to discuss
the obstacles to invoking drala, which must be overcome
before we can master the disciplines of invoking external,
internal, and secret drala. One of the important points in
invoking drala is to prepare a ground of gentleness and genuineness. The basic obstacle to gentleness is arrogance. Arrogance comes from hanging on to the reference point of *me*
and other. You may have studied the principles of warriorship
and Great Eastern Sun vision, and you may have received
numerous teachings on how to rest in nowness and raise your
windhorse, but if you regard those as your personal accomplishment, then you are missing the point. Instead of becoming gentle and tamed, you could become extremely arrogant.
"I, Joe Schmidt, am able to raise windhorse, and *I* feel good
about that. I am beginning to accomplish something, so I am
a big deal."

Being gentle and without arrogance is the Shambhala

definition of a gentleman. According to the *Oxford English Dictionary*, one of the definitions of a gentleman is someone who is not rude, someone whose behavior is gentle and thoroughly trained. However, for the warrior, gentleness is not just politeness. Gentleness is consideration: showing concern for others, all the time. A Shambhala gentlewoman or gentleman is a decent person, a genuine person. He or she is very gentle to himself and to others. The purpose of any protocol, or manners, or discipline that we are taught is to have concern for others. We may think that if we have good manners, we are such good girls or good boys; we know how to eat properly and how to drink properly; we know how to behave properly; and aren't we smart? That is not the point. The point is that, if we have bad table manners, they upset our neighbors, and in turn our neighbors develop bad table manners, and they in turn upset others. If we misuse our napkins and our silverware because we are untrained, that creates problems for others.

Good behavior is not meant to build us up so that we can think of ourselves as little princes or princesses. The point of good behavior is to communicate our respect for others. So we should be concerned with how we behave. When someone enters a room, we should say hello, or stand up and greet them with a handshake. Those rituals are connected with how to have more consideration for others. The principles of warriorship are based on training ourselves and developing self-control so that we can extend ourselves to others. Those disciplines are important in order to cultivate the absence of arrogance.

We tend to think that the threats to our society or to ourselves are outside of us. We fear that some enemy will destroy us. But a society is destroyed from the inside, not from an attack by outsiders. We may imagine the enemy coming with spears and machine guns to kill us, massacre us. In reality, the only thing that can destroy us is within ourselves. If we have too much arrogance, we will destroy our gentleness. And if we destroy gentleness, then we destroy the possibility of being awake, and then we cannot use our intuitive openness to extend ourselves in situations properly. Instead, we generate tremendous aggression.

Aggression desecrates the ground altogether: the ground that you are sitting on, the walls around you, the ceiling and windows and doorways. In turn, you have no place to invite the dralas to come in. The space becomes like an opium den, thick and heavy, and the dralas say, "Yuck, who wants to go in there? Who's inviting us? Who's invoking us with their deception?" They won't come along at all. When the room is filled with *you* and your trip, no sensible person is attracted to that space. Even *you* aren't.

When the environment is stuffy and full of arrogant, self-styled men and women, the dralas are repelled. But then, what happens if a warrior, someone who embodies nonaggression, freedom from arrogance, and humbleness, walks into that room? When such a person enters an intense situation full of arrogance and pollution, quite possibly the occupants of the room begin to feel funny. They feel that they can't have any fun and games anymore, because someone who won't collaborate in their deception has walked in. They can't continue to crack setting-sun jokes or indulge and sprawl on the floor, so usually they will leave. The warrior is left alone, sitting in that room.

But then, after a while, a different group of people may walk in, looking for a fresh room, a clean atmosphere. They begin to assemble—gentle people who smile without arrogance or aggression. The atmosphere is quite different from the previous setting-sun gathering. It may be slightly more rowdy than in the opium den, but the air is cheerful and fresh. Then there is the possibility that the dralas will begin to peek through the doors and the windows. They become interested, and soon they want to come in, and one by one they enter. They accept food and drink, and they relax in that atmosphere, because it is pure and clean. Because that atmosphere is without arrogance, the dralas begin to join in and share their greater sanity.

When the warrior-students experience an environment where the dralas are present, where reality is present, where the possibility of sanity is always there, they can appreciate the mountains, clouds, sky, sunshine, trees, flowers, brooks, the occasional cries and laughter of children. That is the main point of invoking drala: to appreciate reality fully and properly. Arrogant people can't see intensely bright red and blue, brilliant white and orange. Arrogant people are so involved with themselves and they are competing so much with others that they won't even look.

When you are fully gentle, without arrogance and without aggression, you see the brilliance of the universe. You develop a true perception of the universe. You can appreciate green, nicely shaped blades of grass, and you can appreciate striped grasshopper with a tinge of copper color and black antennae. It is so beautiful sitting on a plant. As you walk towards it, it jumps off the plant. Little things like that are not boring sights; they are new discoveries. Every day you see different things. When I was in Texas a few years ago, saw thousands of grasshoppers. Each one of them had its own approach, and they were striped with all sorts of colors. didn't see any purple ones, but I saw copper, green, beige, and black ones, with occasional red spots on them. The world is very interesting wherever you go, wherever you look.

Whatever exists in our world is worth experiencing. Today, perhaps, there is a snowfall. There is snow sitting on the pine trees, and we can watch as the mountains catch the last rays of sun above their deep iron-blue foreground. When we begin to see details of that nature, we feel that the drala principle is there already. We can't ignore the fantastic situations in the phenomenal world. We should actually take the opportunity, seize it on the spot. Invocation of the drala principle comes from that fascination that we have, and that we *should* have—without arrogance. We can appreciate our world, which is so vivid and so beautiful.

FIFTEEN

OVERCOMING HABITUAL PATTERNS

The process of freeing yourself from arrogance and cutting off your habitual tendencies is a very drastic measure, but it is necessary in order to help others in this world.

ARROGANCE comes from lack of gentleness, as we have discussed already. But beyond that, lack of gentleness comes from relying on habitual patterns of behavior. So habitual patterns are also an obstacle to invoking drala. By clinging to habitual behavior, we are cutting ourselves off from the warrior's world. Habitual patterns are almost like reflexes: when we are shocked, we panic, and when we are attacked, we become defensive. On a more subtle level, we use habitual patterns to hide our self-consciousness. When we feel inadequate, we employ habitual responses to patch up our self-image: we invent excuses to shield our inadequacies from other people. Our standard emotional responses are often reflections of habitual patterns, as are mental fatigue, restlessness, irritation over something we don't like, and many of our desires. We use our habitual patterns to seal ourselves off and to build ourselves up.

The Japanese have an interesting term, *toranoko*, which literally means "tiger cub." It is a pejorative term. When you call someone a toranoko, you mean that he is a paper tiger, someone who appears brave but is actually a coward. That is the description of clinging to habitual patterns. You may make feeble attempts to expose your cowardice. Using eloquent language, you may make a confession, saying, "I know I'm not all that fearless," but even your confession is still an expression of toranoko, a fat tiger cub who is afraid of his own shadow, afraid to jump and play with the other cubs.

The Tibetan word for animal is *tudro*. *Tu* means "hunched," and *dro* means "walking." *Tudros* are four-legged animals who walk hunched over. Their most sensitive sense organs are their nostrils, which they use to smell their way through the world. That is a precise description of habitual behavior, which is a manifestation of animal instinct. Habitual patterns allow you to look no further than three steps ahead of you. You are always looking at the ground, and you never look up at the bright blue sky or the mountain peaks. You fail to smile and rejoice at the mist rising off the glaciers. In fact, anything above your shoulder level is embarrassing. No possibility of head and shoulders has ever occurred in that realm.

You may have been instructed in how to experience head and shoulders and how to raise yourself up to see the Great Eastern Sun. But still, if you don't overcome habitual patterns, you could remain a tudro who hunches over and walks on four feet. When you follow your habitual patterns, you never look to the right or to the left, you fail to see the brightness of colors, and you never appreciate the breeze coming in the window. You want to close the window right away, because fresh air is a nuisance.

When a tudro-type person who is filled with habitual patterns looks at a warrior, he might feel that the warrior has a very tedious existence. How in the name of heaven and earth can the warrior be so upright and awake? A tudro, a four-legged, hunched, un-head-and-shouldered person, may feel very sorry for the warrior, because the warrior has to stand on two feet and maintain head and shoulders. Quite possibly such a sympathizer might make a gift of a chair to the warrior, thinking that a chair would make the warrior happy. Then the warrior wouldn't have to maintain his head

94

and shoulders; he could at least slouch once in a while and put his feet on the coffee table.

But a warrior never needs to take time off. Trying to relax by slouching or indulging in habitual patterns only produces schizophrenia. You are such a nice boss and such a good, humorous person at the office, but the minute you come home you forget everything. You turn on your television, you beat your wife, and you send your children to their rooms telling them you need peace and quiet. One wonders what kind of peace and quiet such a person is looking for. It seems rather that he is looking for pain and a hellish life. So you can't be a warrior in the office and a tudro at home.

The process of freeing yourself from arrogance and cutting off your habitual tendencies is a very drastic measure, but it is necessary in order to help others in this world. You should take pride in yourself and uplift yourself. You should regard yourself as an honest and genuine warrior. The former Secretary General of the United Nations, U Thant of Burma, exemplified how to be a warrior and help others without arrogance. He was highly educated and thoroughly soaked in the practice of meditation. He conducted the affairs of the United Nations with dignity, and he was so soft and gentle. Therefore people felt in awe of him; they felt his power. They admired what he said, and the decisions he made. He was one of the great statesmen of this century and a great example of someone who has overcome habitual patterns.

Habitual patterns are dangerous and destructive. They prevent you from seeing the Great Eastern Sun. When habitual patterns constantly operate, you can't raise up your head and shoulders at all. You are down there, looking down, looking for this and that. You are more concerned with the flies sitting on your cup than with the great sun that is coming up. You have forgotten about uplifted and open vision, and about seeing the Great Eastern Sun directly; you begin to dissolve yourself, and involve yourself in a subhuman or even subanimal realm. You are not willing to take part in any immediate delight. You are not willing to relate with the least edge of pain, or even discomfort, in order to see the Great Eastern Sun.

When you were very young, three years old, you didn't

95

want to escape reality, particularly, because you were so interested in how things were done. You used to ask your father and mother all sorts of questions: "Why is this so, Mommy? Why is this so, Daddy? Why do we do this? Why don't we do that?" But that innocent inquisitiveness has been forgotten, lost. Therefore, you have to reignite it. Entering the cocoon of tudro behavior happens after that initial inquisitiveness. Once there was tremendous inquisitiveness, and then you thought that you were being mistreated by your world, so you jumped into your cocoon and decided to sleep.

Uplifting your head and shoulders may sometimes give you back pains or a strained neck, but extending yourself, uplifting yourself, is necessary. We are not talking about philosophy, but we are talking about how on earth, how in the name of heaven and earth, we can actually become decent human beings without trying to entertain ourselves from here to the next corner. The constant search for immediate entertainment is a big problem. "What can I do next? How can I save myself from boredom? I don't want to see that bright world at all." As we sew our fabric with a needle and thread, we think, "Is there another way that I can make these stitches? Is there any way that I can avoid having to make a straight journey?" The journey we are making is demanding, but there is no way of avoiding it.

By stopping habitual patterns, we can appreciate the real world on the spot. We can appreciate the bright, beautiful fantastic world around us; we don't have to feel all that resentful or embarrassed. If we don't negate our habitual patterns, we can never fully appreciate the world. But once we overcome habitual patterns, the vividness of the drala principle, the magic, will descend, and we will begin to be individual masters of our world.

SIXTEEN

SACRED WORLD

> *When human beings lose their connection to nature, to heaven and earth, then they do not know how to nurture their environment or how to rule their world—which is saying the same thing. Human beings destroy their ecology at the same time that they destroy one another. From that perspective, healing our society goes hand in hand with healing our personal, elemental connection with the phenomenal world.*

ARROGANCE AND HABITUAL PATTERNS, as we discussed in the last two chapters, are obstacles to experiencing drala. In order to discover magic in the world, we have to overcome the individual neurosis and self-centered attitudes that prevent us from experiencing greater vision beyond ourselves. By obscuring our vision, they also prevent us from uplifting ourselves so that we can extend ourselves to help others.

Some people feel that the world's problems are so pressing that social and political action should take precedence over individual development. They may feel that they should sacrifice their own needs completely in order to work for a larger cause. In its extreme form, this kind of thinking justifies individual neurosis and aggression as purely a product of a troubled society, so that people feel they can hold onto their neurosis and even use their aggression to try to effect change.

According to the Shambhala teachings, however, we have to recognize that our individual experience of sanity is inherently linked to our vision for a good human society. So we have to take things one step at a time. If we try to solve society's problems without overcoming the confusion and aggression in our own state of mind, then our efforts will only contribute to the basic problems, instead of solving them. That is why the individual journey of warriorship must be undertaken before we can address the larger issue of how to help this world. Still, it would be extremely unfortunate if Shambhala vision were taken as purely another attempt to build ourselves up while ignoring our responsibilities to others. The point of warriorship is to become a gentle and tamed human being who can make a genuine contribution to this world. The warrior's journey is based on discovering what is intrinsically good about human existence and how to share that basic nature of goodness with others. There is a natural order and harmony to this world, which we can discover. But we cannot just study that order scientifically or measure it mathematically. We have to feel it—in our bones, in our hearts, in our minds. If we are thoroughly trained in the disciplines of warriorship, then by invoking the drala principle, we can reawaken that intimate connection to reality. That provides the ground to work with others in a genuine and gentle fashion.

When you invoke drala, you begin to experience basic goodness reflected everywhere—in yourself, in others, and in the entire world. You are not being blind to the setting-sun or degraded aspects of existence. In fact, you see them very precisely, because you are so alert. But you also see that every aspect of life has the potential of being upgraded, that there is the potential for sacredness in every situation. So you begin to view the universe as a sacred world. The sacred world is that which exists spontaneously, naturally in the phenomenal world. When you have gold, that gold can be formed into different shapes—both beautiful and grotesque— but it still remains twenty-four carat gold. A diamond may be worn by the most degraded person, but it still remains a diamond.

Similarly, the idea of sacred world is that, although you see the confusion and problems that fill the world, you also see that phenomenal existence is constantly being influenced by the vision of the Great Eastern Sun. In fact, we could say that it takes on the qualities of the Great Eastern Sun. The sacred world is *Great* because of its primordial quality. That is, sacredness goes back and back through history to prehistory to before history, before thought, before mind had ever thought of anything at all. So experiencing the greatness of the sacred world is recognizing the existence of that vast and primordial wisdom, which is reflected throughout phenomena. This wisdom is old and young at the same time, and it is never tarnished or diminished by the relative problems in the world.

The sacred world is connected with *East*, because there are always possibilities of vision in this world. East represents the dawn of wakefulness, the horizon of human consciousness where vision is constantly arising. Wherever you are, when you open your eyes, you always look ahead, to the East. You always have possibilities of wakeful vision, even in the most degraded or confused situations. Finally, the sacred world is lighted by the *Sun*, which is the principle of never-ending brilliance and radiance. The sun is also connected with seeing self-existing possibilities of virtue and richness in the world. Normally, when you see a brilliant light, that light comes from a finite source of energy. The brightness of a candle depends on how much wax surrounds it and the thickness of the wick. The brightness of a light bulb depends on the electric current running through it. But the Great Eastern Sun is eternally blazing: it has no need of fuel. There actually is greater luminosity that occurs without fuel, without even a pilot light. Seeing the sacred world is witnessing that greater vision, which is there all the time.

The experience of sacred world begins to show you how you are woven together with the richness and brilliance of the phenomenal world. You are a natural part of that world, and you begin to see possibilities of natural hierarchy or natural order, which could provide the model for how to conduct your life. Ordinarily, hierarchy is regarded in the negative sense as a ladder or a vertical power structure, with power concentrated at the top. If you are on the bottom rungs of that ladder, then you feel oppressed by what is above you and you try to abolish it, or you try to climb higher on the ladder. But for the warrior, discovering hierarchy is seeing the Great Eastern Sun reflected everywhere in everything. You see possibilities of order in the world that are not based on struggle and aggression. In other words, you perceive a way to be in harmony with the phenomenal world that is neither static nor repressive. So the understanding of hierarchy manifests as a sense of natural decorum, or knowing how to behave. That is, you see how to *be* naturally in this world, because you experience dignity and elegance that do not have to be cultivated.

The warrior's decorum is this natural togetherness and calm, which come from a feeling of being in harmony with yourself and with the environment. You don't have to try to fit yourself into situations, but situations fit naturally. When you achieve this level of decorum, then you can abandon the final vestiges of the giant backpack of habitual patterns that you have been carrying for so long to protect yourself from nature. You can appreciate nature's own qualities, and you see that you do not need your bag of ego-centered tricks. You realize that you can live with nature, as it is, and as you are. You feel a sense of ease or looseness. You feel at home in your world.

In that way, the invocation of the drala principle allows us to live in harmony with the elemental quality of reality. The modern approach often seems to be one of trying to conquer the elements. There is central heating to conquer winter's cold, and air conditioning to conquer summer's heat. When there is drought or flooding or a hurricane, it is seen as a battle with the elements, as an uncomfortable reminder of their strength. The warrior's approach is that, rather than trying to overcome the raw elements of existence, one should respect their power and their order as a guide to human conduct. In the ancient philosophies of both China and Japan, the three principles of heaven, earth, and man expressed this view of how human life and society could be integrated with the order of the natural world. These principles are based on an ancient understanding of natural hierarchy. I have found that, in presenting the discipline of warriorship, the principles of heaven, earth, and man are very helpful in describing how the warrior should take his seat in the sacred world. Although politically and socially, our values are quite different from those of Imperial China and Japan, it is still possible to appreciate the basic wisdom contained in these principles of natural order.

Heaven, earth, and man can be seen literally as the sky above, the earth below, and human beings standing or sitting between the two. Unfortunately, the use of "man" here, rather than "human being," may have a limiting connotation for some readers. (By "man," in this case, we simply mean anthropomorphic existence—human existence—not man as opposed to woman.) Traditionally, heaven is the realm of the gods, the most sacred space. So, symbolically, the principle of heaven represents any lofty ideal or experience of vastness and sacredness. The grandeur and vision of heaven are what inspire human greatness and creativity. Earth, on the other hand, symbolizes practicality and receptivity. It is the ground that supports and promotes life. Earth may seem solid and stubborn, but earth can be penetrated and worked on. Earth can be cultivated. The proper relationship between heaven and earth is what makes the earth principle pliable. You might think of the space of heaven as very dry and conceptual, but warmth and love also come from heaven. Heaven is the source of the rain that falls on the earth, so heaven has a sympathetic connection with earth. When that connection is made, then the earth begins to yield. It becomes gentle and soft and pliable, so that greenery can grow on it, and man can cultivate it.

Then there is the man principle, which is connected with simplicity, or living in harmony with heaven and earth. When human beings combine the freedom of heaven with the practicality of earth, they can live in a good human society with one another. Traditionally it is said that, when human beings live in harmony with the principles of heaven and earth, then the four seasons and the elements of the world will also work together harmoniously. Then there is no fear and human beings begin to join in, as they deserve, in living in this world. They have heaven above and earth below, and they appreciate the trees and the greenery and so on. They begin to appreciate all this.

But if human beings violate their connection, or lose

their trust in heaven and earth, then there will be social chaos and natural disasters. In Chinese the character for the ruler, or king, is a vertical line joining three horizontal lines, which represent heaven, earth, and man. This means that the king has the power to join heaven and earth in a good human society. Traditionally, if there was plenty of rainfall, and crops and vegetation flourished, then this indicated that the king was genuine, that he truly joined heaven and earth. But when there was drought and starvation or natural catastrophes, such as flooding and earthquakes, then the power of the king was in doubt. The idea that harmony in nature is linked to harmony in human affairs is not purely an Oriental concept. For example, there are many stories in the Bible, such as the story of King David, that portray the conflict between heaven and earth and the doubt that it raises about the king.

If we apply the perspective of heaven, earth, and man to the situation in the world today, we begin to see that there is a connection between the social and the natural, or environmental, problems that we are facing. When human beings lose their connection to nature, to heaven and earth, then they do not know how to nurture their environment or how to rule their world—which is saying the same thing. Human beings destroy their ecology at the same time that they destroy one another. From that perspective, healing our society goes hand in hand with healing our personal, elemental connection with the phenomenal world.

When human beings have no sense of living with a wide open sky above and a lush green earth below, then it becomes very difficult for them to expand their vision. When we feel that heaven is an iron lid and that earth is a parched desert, then we want to hide away rather than extending ourselves to help others. Shambhala vision does not reject technology or simplistically advocate going "back to nature." But within the world that we live in, there is room to relax and appreciate ourselves and our heaven and our earth. We can afford to love ourselves, and we can afford to raise our head and shoulders to see the bright sun shining in the sky.

The challenge of warriorship is to live fully in the world as it is and to find within this world, with all its paradoxes,

the essence of nowness. If we open our eyes, if we open our minds, if we open our hearts, we will find that this world is a magical place. It is not magical because it tricks us or changes unexpectedly into something else, but it is magical because it can *be* so vividly, so brilliantly. However, the discovery of that magic can happen only when we transcend our embarrassment about being alive, when we have the bravery to proclaim the goodness and dignity of human life, without either hesitation or arrogance. Then magic, or drala, can descend onto our existence.

The world is filled with power and wisdom, which we can have, so to speak. In some sense we have them already. By invoking the drala principle, we have possibilities of experiencing the sacred world, a world which has self-existing richness and brilliance—and beyond that, possibilities of natural hierarchy, natural order. That order includes all the aspects of life—including those that are ugly and bitter and sad. But even those qualities are part of the rich fabric of existence that can be woven into our being. In fact, we are woven already into that fabric—whether we like it or not. Recognizing that link is both powerful and auspicious. It allows us to stop complaining about and fighting with our world. Instead, we can begin to celebrate and promote the sacredness of the world. By following the way of the warrior, it is possible to expand our vision and give fearlessly to others. In that way, we have possibilities of effecting fundamental change. We cannot change the way the world *is*, but by opening ourselves to the world *as it is*, we may find that gentleness, decency, and bravery are available—not only to us, but to all human beings.

SEVENTEEN

NATURAL HIERARCHY

> *Living in accordance with natural hierarchy is not a matter of following a series of rigid rules or structuring your days with lifeless commandments or codes of conduct. The world has order and power and richness that can teach you how to conduct your life artfully, with kindness to others and care for yourself.*

THE PRINCIPLES OF HEAVEN, EARTH, AND MAN that were discussed in the last chapter are one way of describing natural hierarchy. They are a way of viewing the order of the cosmic world: the greater world of which all human beings are a part. In this chapter, I would like to present another way of seeing this order, which is part of the Shambhala wisdom of my native country of Tibet. This view of the world is also divided into three parts, which are called *lha*, *nyen*, and *lu*. These three principles are not in conflict with the principles of heaven, earth, and man, but as you will see, they are a slightly different perspective. Lha, nyen, and lu are more rooted in the laws of the earth, although they acknowledge the command of heaven and the place of human beings. Lha, nyen, and lu describe the protocol and the decorum of the earth itself, and they show how human beings can weave themselves into that texture of basic reality. So the application of the lha, nyen, and lu principles is actually a further way to invoke the power of drala or elemental magic.

105

Lha literally means "divine" or "god," but in this case, lha refers to the highest points on earth, rather than a celestial realm. The realm of lha is the peaks of snow mountains, where glaciers and bare rock are found. Lha is the highest point, the point that catches the light of the rising sun first of all. It is the places on earth that reach into the heavens above, into the clouds; so lha is as close to the heavens as the earth can reach.

Psychologically, lha represents the first wakefulness. It is the experience of tremendous freshness and freedom from pollution in your state of mind. Lha is what reflects the Great Eastern Sun for the first time in your being and it is also the sense of shining out, projecting tremendous goodness. In the body, lha is the head, especially your eyes and forehead, so it represents physical upliftedness and projecting out as well.

Then, there is *nyen*, which literally means "friend." Nyen begins with the great shoulders of the mountains, and includes forests, jungles and plains. A mountain peak is lha, but the dignified shoulders of the mountain are nyen. In the Japanese samurai tradition, the large starched shoulders on the warriors' uniforms represent nyen principle. And in the Western military tradition, epaulets that accentuate the shoulders play the same role. In the body, nyen includes not only your shoulders but your torso, your chest and rib cage. Psychologically, it is solidity, feeling solidly grounded in goodness, grounded in the earth. So nyen is connected with bravery and the gallantry of human beings. In that sense, it is an enlightened version of friendship: being courageous and helpful to others.

Finally, there is *lu*, which literally means "water being." It is the realm of oceans and rivers and great lakes, the realm of water and wetness. Lu has the quality of a liquid jewel, so wetness is connected here with richness. Psychologically, the experience of lu is like jumping into a gold lake. Lu is also freshness, but it is not quite the same as the freshness of the glacier mountains of lha. Here, freshness is like sunlight reflecting in a deep pool of water, showing the liquid jewellike quality of the water. In your body, lu is your legs and feet: everything below your waist.

Lha, nyen, and lu are also related to the seasons. Winter

is lha; it is the loftiest season of all. In the winter, you feel as if you were upstairs, above the clouds; it is cold and crisp, as if you were flying in the sky. Then there is spring, which is coming down from heaven and beginning to contact earth. Spring is a transition from lha to nyen. Then there is summer, which is the fully developed level of nyen, when things are green, in full bloom. And then summer develops into autumn, which is related with lu, because fruition takes place, the final development. The fruit and harvest of the autumn are the fruition of lu. In the rhythm of the four seasons, lha, nyen, and lu interact with one another in a developmental process. This applies to many other situations. The interaction of lha, nyen, and lu is like snow melting on a mountain. The sun warms the peaks of the mountain, and the glaciers and snow begin to melt. That is lha. Then the water runs down the mountainside to form streams and rivers, which is nyen. Finally, the rivers converge in the ocean, which is lu, the fruition.

The interaction of lha, nyen, and lu also can be seen in human interactions and behavior. For example, money is lha principle; establishing a bank account and depositing your money in the bank is nyen; and drawing money out of the bank to pay your bills or to buy something is lu. Or another example is as simple as having a drink of water. You can't drink water out of an empty glass, so first you pour water into the glass, which is the place of lha. Then you pick up the glass in your hands, which is nyen. And finally you drink, which is the place of lu.

Lha, nyen, and lu play a role in every situation in life. Every object you handle is connected with one of those three places. For example, in terms of clothing, the hat is in the place of lha, the shoes are in the place of lu, and shirts, dresses and trousers are in the place of nyen. If you mix up those principles, then you instinctively know that something is wrong. For instance, if the sun is beating on your head, you don't put your shoes on your head as a visor to protect you from the sun. And on the other hand, you don't walk on your eyeglasses. You don't stuff your shoes with your ties and, for that matter, you shouldn't put your feet on the table, because it is mixing up lu and nyen. Personal articles that belong to the lha realm include hats, glasses, earrings, toothbrushes, and hairbrushes. Articles belonging to the realm of nyen are rings, belts, ties, shirts and blouses, cuff links, bracelets, and watches. Articles belonging to the place of lu include shoes and socks and underwear. I'm afraid it is as literal as that. Lha, nyen, and lu are quite straightforward and very ordinary.

Observing the order of lha, nyen, and lu is what makes human beings civilized, and therefore we might refer to them as the ultimate protocol. By following the order of lha, nyen, and lu, your life can be harmonized with the order of the phenomenal world. Some people would like to ignore such basic societal norms. They say: "So what if I put my shoes on my head?" But everybody knows that something is not quite right in doing that, although nobody knows exactly why. People have an instinct that prompts them to have a place for each article of clothing or household belonging. Those norms actually make sense. Your bedroom and your entire house are much tidier if you put certain belongings in certain places. From that, you develop rhythm and order in your experience. You do not throw your garments on the floor, you do not put your slippers under your pillow, and you do not use your hairbrush to polish your shoes.

Ignoring the order of lha, nyen, and lu is very destructive. If instead of winter, summer followed autumn, and if instead of autumn, spring followed summer, the whole order of cosmic principles would be violated. In that case, crops wouldn't grow, animals wouldn't reproduce, and we would have devastating droughts and floods. When the order of lha, nyen, and lu is violated in society, it is like disrupting the order of the seasons: it weakens society and causes confusion.

Sometimes you see the violation of lha, nyen, and lu reflected in the actions of political leaders: the president of the United States putting his feet on the desk of the Oval Office, or the famous incident of Premier Khrushchev pounding his shoe on the United Nations' podium. It is not that those actions in themselves are the real problem. Incorporating the law of lha, nyen, and lu is more than just having good manners. What is truly problematic is the attitude that violates the sacredness of life: thinking that the way to make a forceful statement is to turn the world topsy-turvy by ignoring its basic norms. You lose your trust in the phenomenal world, and at the same time, you become an untrustworthy person yourself, someone who thinks that wheeling and dealing his way through life is the road to success. Maybe there is some temporary victory in that kind of approach, but ultimately you are throwing yourself into the gutter of the world.

So respecting the order of lha, nyen, and lu is very important. This does not mean just paying lip service to those principles by having an orderly household with everything in its place. You begin by appreciating your world, by taking a fresh look at the universe, which we have discussed over and over. Then, out of that, you feel the presence of lha, nyen, and lu in your body, your entire being. You feel the wakefulness and vision of lha, the solidity and gentleness of nyen, and the rich possibilities of treading the earth, which are lu principle. Then, from that discovery of basic decorum, you begin to understand how to join the lha, nyen, and lu principles together by giving yourself to others, by serving your world.

Joining lha, nyen, and lu is exemplified in the act of bowing, which in many Oriental cultures is a traditional greeting. For the Shambhala warrior, the bow is a symbol of surrendering to others, serving them. We are not talking here just about the literal act of bowing, but about the warrior's whole attitude towards his or her life, which is one of selfless service. When as a warrior you make a bow, you begin by establishing your head and shoulders, uplifting your posture. You don't just roar in and bow, but first you hold yourself erect. This connects you with the realm of lha and with raising windhorse. It is as if you had glaciers on your head, as if you were Mount Everest. Then, from that cutting and fresh glacier mountain realm of lha, you begin to bend down by lowering your head and hunching slightly. You give to your shoulders from your head. This is making friends with nyen: you acknowledge the breadth and vastness of your shoulders. Then finally, you complete your bow. You submit to the realm of lu. You completely surrender. Your entire three systems of lha, nyen, and lu are offered as you bend down.

Bowing is giving away basic goodness and windhorse to

others. So in bowing you are surrendering potential power and magic, and you do that with real, proper feeling. It is a threefold process: hold, feel, and give. First you have to hold; otherwise you don't make any statement. If you bow to someone by just flopping down, that is a very gullible bow. It does not have any heart to it. The witnesser of that bow, the person you bow to, will regard you as an untrustworthy person. The idea is that the magic of the bow, the power of the bow, actually confirms both people. When you bow to your friend or to a good, trustworthy person who also possesses that power, then you are sharing something together. If you bow to the setting sun, if you bow to Mickey Mouse, you are degrading yourself. The warrior never does that. So the bow is based on acknowledging someone else's worth, his or her lha, nyen, and lu existing in front of you. And, as a mark of respect, you do not rise from your bow until the other person rises.

The bow represents a complementary exchange of energy, as well as being a mark of decency, loyalty, and surrender. It is both an example and an analogy of how to join lha, nyen, and lu together. Basically, the point is to serve the world. Tools, which help us to shape our world, are also regarded as joining lha, nyen, and lu and should be given special respect. The same is true for human beings who help to shape the lives of others by serving them. So a teacher is highly respected, because he or she is joining lha, nyen, and lu in the students. Ideally, politicians and public servants also have this role. The role of the warrior altogether is to join lha, nyen, and lu in order to help his or her fellow human beings.

Living in accordance with natural hierarchy is not a matter of following a series of rigid rules or structuring your days with lifeless commandments or codes of conduct. The world has order and power and richness that can teach you how to conduct your life artfully, with kindness to others and care for yourself. However, just studying the principles of lha, nyen, and lu is not enough. The discovery of natural hierarchy has to be a personal experience—magic is something you must experience for yourself. Then, you will never be tempted to put your hat on the floor, but more importantly, you will never be tempted to cheat your neighbors or your friends. You will be inspired to serve your world, to surrender yourself completely.

EIGHTEEN

HOW TO RULE

The notion of ruling your world is that you can live in a dignified and disciplined way, without frivolity, and at the same time enjoy your life. You can combine survival and celebration.

THE WARRIOR'S JOURNEY of discovering the natural hierarchy of reality and his place in that world is both exalted and very simple. It is simple, because it is so immediate and touching. It is touching your origin—your place in this world, the place you came from and the place you belong. It is as if you were taking a long walk through the woods at twilight. You hear the sounds of birds and catch a glimpse of the fading light in the sky. You see a crescent moon and clusters of stars. You appreciate the freshness of the greenery and the beauty of wild flowers. In the distance dogs are barking, children are crying, and occasionally you hear the sound of a car or truck making its journey on the highway. As the wind begins to blow on your cheeks, you smell the freshness of the woodlands, and perhaps you startle an occasional rabbit or bird as you pass them by. As twilight goes on, memories of your husband, your wife, your children, your grandparents, your world, come back to you. You remember your first schoolroom, where you learned to spell and read and write. You

112

remember tracing the letters *i* and *o, m* and *a*. You are walking in the forest of the dralas, but still there is a feeling that this woodland is surrounded by other living human beings. Yet, when you listen, you hear only the sound of your own footsteps—right, left, right, left, a crackle when you step on a dry twig.

When you walk into this world of reality, the greater or cosmic world, you will find the way to rule your world—but, at the same time, you will also find a deep sense of aloneness. It is possible that this world could become a palace or a kingdom to you, but as its king or queen, you will be a monarch with a broken heart. It is not a bad thing to be, by any means. In fact, it is the way to be a decent human being—and beyond that a glorious human being who can help others.

This kind of aloneness is painful, but at the same time, it is beautiful and real. Out of such painful sadness, a longing and a willingness to work with others will come naturally. You realize that you are unique. You see that there is something good about being you as yourself. Because you care for yourself, you begin to care for others who have nurtured your existence or have made their own journey of warriorship, paving the way for you to travel this path. Therefore, you feel dedication and devotion to the lineage of warriors, brave people, whoever they have been, who have made this same journey. And at the same time, you begin to care for all those who have yet to take this path. Because you have seen that it is possible for you, you realize that you can help others to do the same.

You begin to see that there are seasons in your life in the same way as there are seasons in nature. There are times to cultivate and create, when you nurture your world and give birth to new ideas and ventures. There are times of flourishing and abundance, when life feels in full bloom, energized and expanding. And there are times of fruition, when things come to an end. They have reached their climax and must be harvested before they begin to fade. And finally, of course, there are times that are cold and cutting and empty, times when the spring of new beginnings seems like a distant dream. Those rhythms in life are natural events. They weave into one another as day follows night, bringing, not messages of hope and fear, but messages of how things *are*. If you realize that each phase of your life is a natural occurrence, then you need not be swayed, pushed up and down by the changes in circumstance and mood that life brings. You find that you have an opportunity to be fully in the world at all times and to show yourself as a brave and proud individual in any circumstance.

Normally, there appears to be a conflict between survival and celebration. Survival, taking care of your basic needs, is based on pragmatism, exertion, and often drudgery. Celebration, on the other hand, is often connected with extravagance and doing something beyond your means. The notion of ruling your world is that you can live in a dignified and disciplined way, without frivolity, and at the same time enjoy your life. You can combine survival and celebration. The kingdom that you are ruling is your own life: it is a householder's kingdom. Whether or not you have a husband or wife and children, still there is a structure and pattern to your daily life. Many people feel that the regularity of life is a constant imposition. They would like to have a different life, or a different menu, every second, at every meal. It is necessary to settle down somewhere and work at having a regular, disciplined life. The more discipline that occurs, however, the more joyous life can be. So the pattern of your life can be a joyous one, a celebration, rather than obligation alone. That is what it means to rule the kingdom of your life.

The notion of kingdom here is that your life is potentially wealthy and good. There is a great deal of misunderstanding about wealth. Generally being wealthy means that you have lots of money, but the real meaning of wealth is knowing how to create a goldlike situation in your life. That is to say, you may have only twenty dollars in your bank account, but you can still manifest richness in your world.

Interestingly, if you are lost in the desert, without food and water, even if you have lots of gold in your pack, you can't eat it and you can't drink it—so you are still starved and parched. That is analogous to what happens to many people who have money. They have no idea how to eat it and how to drink it. Once I heard a story about an Indian chief who struck oil on his property and became rich. He decided to buy twenty basins and bath taps at once as a sign of his wealth. People can spend thousands of dollars and still be dissatisfied and in tremendous pain. Even with all that supposed wealth, they may still be unable to enjoy a simple meal.

True wealth does not come about automatically. It has to be cultivated; you have to earn it. Otherwise, even if you have lots of money, you will still be starved. So if you want to rule your world, please don't think that means you have to spend a great deal of money. Rather, true wealth comes from using manpower, individual power. If your suit has lots of lint, don't send it to the cleaners right away—clean it yourself. That is much less expensive, and also more dignified. You put your own energy and effort into caring for your world. The key to wealth, or the golden key, is appreciating that you can be poor—or I should say, unmoneyed—and still feel good, because you have a sense of wealthiness in any case, already. That is the wonderful key to richness and the first step in ruling: appreciating that wealth and richness come from being a basically decent human being. You do not have to be jealous of those who have more, in an economic sense, than you do. You can be rich even if you are poor.

That twist is a very interesting one and very powerful in terms of how to deal with world problems. Too often the politics of this world are based on poverty. If people are poor, they want to take money or resources away from those who have more. And if people are wealthy—in the sense of having money—then they want to hold onto what they have, because they think that giving up some of their money will make them impoverished. With that mentality on both sides, it is difficult to imagine any fundamental change taking place. Or if it does take place, it is based on tremendous hatred and violence, because both sides are hanging on so tightly to what they think is important.

Of course, if you are starving, then what you want is food. In fact, food is what you need. But the genuine desires of those who are in need can be ruthlessly manipulated. War based on grasping has happened over and over again in this world. People with money have been willing to sacrifice thousands of human lives to hold onto their wealth, and on the other side, people in need have been willing to massacre their fellows for a grain of rice, a hope for a penny in their pocket.

Mahatma Gandhi asked the Indian people to embrace nonviolence and to renounce clinging to foreign ways, which they associated with wealth and prosperity. Since most Indians wore cloth that was British-made, he asked them to give up wearing British cloth and weave their own. This proclamation of self-sufficiency was one way, and a powerful one, of promoting dignity based, not on material possessions, but on one's inherent state of being. But at the same time, with every respect for Gandhi's vision of nonaggression, which he called *satyagraha*, or "seizing the truth," we should not confuse his message with extreme asceticism. In order to find one's inherent wealth, it is not necessary to renounce all material possessions and worldly pursuits. If a society is to have a sense of command and being ruled, then someone has to wear the three-piece suit at the negotiating tables; someone has to wear a uniform to keep the peace.

The basic message of the Shambhala teachings is that the best of human life can be realized under ordinary circumstances. That is the basic wisdom of Shambhala: that in this world, as it is, we can find a good and meaningful human life that will also serve others. That is our true richness. At a time when the world faces the threat of nuclear destruction and the reality of mass starvation and poverty, ruling our lives means committing ourselves to live in this world as ordinary but fully human beings. The image of the warrior in the world is indeed, precisely, this.

In a practical sense, how can we bring the sense of richness and ruling into our ordinary lives? When the warrior has achieved a certain mentality, having understood the basic principles of dignity and gentleness thoroughly, as well as having an appreciation for the drala principle and the principles of lha, nyen, and lu, then he or she should reflect on the general sense of wealth or richness in his life. The basic practice of richness is learning to project the goodness that exists in your being, so that a sense of general goodness shines out. That goodness can be reflected in the way your hair is combed, the way your suit fits, the way your living room looks—in whatever there is in your immediate world. Then it is possible to go further and experience greater richness by developing what are called the seven riches of the universal monarch. These are very ancient categories first used in India to describe the qualities of a ruler. In this case, we are talking about developing these qualities individually, personally.

The first richness of the ruler is to have a queen. The queen—or we could say wife or husband, if you like—represents the principle of decency in your household. When you live with someone with whom you can share your life, both your wisdom and your negativities, it encourages you to open up your personality. You don't bottle things up. However, a Shambhala person does not have to be married. There is always room for bachelors. Bachelors are friends to themselves as well as having a circle of friends. The basic principle is to develop decency and reasonability in your relationships.

The second richness of the universal monarch is the minister. The principle of the minister is having a counselor. You have your spouse who promotes your decency, and then you have friends who provide counsel and advice. It is said that the ministers should be inscrutable. The sense of inscrutability here is not that your friends are devious or difficult to figure out but that they do not have a project or goal in mind that clouds their friendship with you. Their advice or help is open-ended.

The third richness is the general, who represents fearlessness and protection. The general is also a friend, a friend who is fearless because he or she has no resistance to protecting you and helping you out, doing whatever is needed in a situation. The general is a friend who will actually care for you, as opposed to one who provides counsel.

The fourth richness is the steed, or horse. The steed represents industriousness, working hard and exerting yourself in situations. You don't get trapped in laziness, but you constantly go forward and work with situations in your life.

The fifth richness is the elephant, which represents steadiness. You are not swayed by the winds of deception or confusion. You are steady like an elephant. At the same time, an elephant is not rooted like a tree trunk—it walks and moves. So you can walk and move forward with steadiness, as though riding an elephant.

The sixth richness of the ruler is the wish-granting jewel, which is connected with generosity. You don't just hold onto the richness that you achieve by applying the previous principles, but you let go and give—by being hospitable, open, and humorous.

Number seven is the wheel. Traditionally, the ruler of the entire universe holds a gold wheel, while the monarch who rules this earth alone receives an iron wheel. The rulers of Shambhala are said to have held the iron wheel, because they ruled on this earth. On a personal level, the wheel represents command over your world. You take your seat properly and fully in your life, so that all of the previous principles can work together to promote richness and dignity in your life.

By applying these seven principles of richness, you can actually handle your family life properly. You have a wife or husband, which promotes decency; you have close friends, who are your advisers; and you have your guardians, or companions, who are fearless in loving you. Then you have exertion in your journey, in your work, which is represented by the horse. You ride on your energy all the time; you never give up on any of the problems in your life. But at the same time, you have to be earthy, steady, like an elephant. Then, having all those, you don't just feel self-satisfied, but you become generous to others, like the wish-granting gem. Because of that, you rule your household completely; you hold the wheel of command. That is the vision of how to run your household in an enlightened fashion.

Having done that, you feel that your life is established properly and fully. You feel that a golden rain is continuously descending. It feels solid, simple, and straightforward. Then, you also have a feeling of gentleness and openness, as though an exquisite flower has bloomed auspiciously in your life. In whatever action you perform, whether accepting or rejecting, you begin to open yourself to the treasury of Shambhala wisdom. The point is that, when there is harmony, then there is also fundamental wealth. Although at that particular

118

point you might be penniless, there is no problem. You are suddenly, eternally rich.

If you want to solve the world's problems, you have to put your own household, your own individual life, in order first. That is somewhat of a paradox. People have a genuine desire to go beyond their individual, cramped lives to benefit the world. But if you do not start at home, then you have no hope of helping the world. So the first step in learning how to rule is learning to rule your household, your immediate world. There is no doubt that, if you do so, then the next step will come naturally. If you fail to do so, then your contribution to this world will be further chaos.

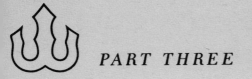 *PART THREE*

AUTHENTIC PRESENCE

For the dignified Shambhala person,
An unwaning authentic presence dawns.

NINETEEN

THE UNIVERSAL MONARCH

The challenge of warriorship is to step out of the cocoon, to step out into space, by being brave and at the same time gentle.

IN PART TWO we discussed the possibility of discovering magic, or drala, and how that discovery can allow us to transform our existence into an expression of sacred world. Although, in some respects, all of these teachings are based on very simple and ordinary experiences, at the same time, you might feel somewhat overwhelmed by this perspective, as though you were surrounded by monumental wisdom. You still might have questions about how to go about actualizing the vision of warriorship.

Is it simply your personal will power and exertion which bring about the courage to follow the path of the Shambhala warriors? Or do you just imagine that you are seeing the Great Eastern Sun and hope for the best—that what you have seen is "it"? Neither of these will work. We have seen in the past that some people try to become warriors with an intense push. But the result is further confusion, and the person uncovers layer upon layer of cowardice and incompetence. If there is no sense of rejoicing and magical practice, you find yourself simply driving into the high wall of insanity.

The way of the warrior, how to be a warrior, is not a matter of making amateurish attempts, hoping that one day you will be a professional. There is a difference between imitating and emulating. In emulating warriorship, the student of warriorship goes through stages of disciplined training and constantly looks back and re-examines his own footprints or handiwork. Sometimes you find signs of development, and sometimes you find signs that you missed the point. Nevertheless, this is the only way to actualize the path of the warrior.

The fruition of the warrior's path is the experience of primordial goodness, or the complete, unconditional nature of basic goodness. This experience is the same as the complete realization of egolessness, or the truth of non-reference point. The discovery of non-reference point, however, comes only from working with the reference points that exist in your life. By reference points here, we simply mean all of the conditions and situations that are part of your journey through life: washing your clothes, eating breakfast, lunch, and dinner, paying bills. Your week starts with Monday, and then you have Tuesday, Wednesday, Thursday, Friday, Saturday, and Sunday. You get up at six A.M. and then the morning passes and you have noon, afternoon, evening, and night. You know what time to get up, what time to take a shower, what time to go to work, what time to eat dinner, and what time to lie down and go to sleep. Even a simple act like drinking a cup of tea contains many reference points. You pour yourself a cup of tea; you pick up a spoonful of sugar and bring it towards your teacup; you dip the spoon into the cup and stir it around so that the sugar becomes thoroughly mixed with the tea; you put the spoon down; you pick up the cup by its handle and bring it towards your mouth; you drink a little bit of tea and then you put the cup down. All of those processes are simple and ordinary reference points that show you how to conduct your journey through life.

Then you have reference points that are connected with how you express your emotions. You have love affairs, you have quarrels, and sometimes you get bored with life, so you read a newspaper or watch television. All of those emotional textures provide reference points in conducting your life.

The principles of warriorship are concerned, first of all, with learning to appreciate those processes, those mundane reference points. But then, by relating with the ordinary conditions of your life, you might make a shocking discovery. While drinking your cup of tea, you might discover that you are drinking tea in a vacuum. In fact, *you* are not even drinking the tea. The hollowness of space is drinking tea. So while doing any little ordinary thing, that reference point might bring an experience of non-reference point. When you put on your pants or your skirt, you might find that you are dressing up space. When you put on your make-up, you might discover that you are putting cosmetics on space. You are beautifying space, pure nothingness.

In the ordinary sense, we think of space as something vacant or dead. But in this case, space is a vast world that has capabilities of absorbing, acknowledging, and accommodating. You can put cosmetics on it, drink tea with it, eat cookies with it, polish your shoes in it. Something is there. But ironically, if you look into it, you can't find anything. If you try to put your finger on it, you find that you don't even have a finger to put! That is the primordial nature of basic goodness, and it is that nature which allows a human being to become a warrior, to become the warrior of all warriors.

The warrior, fundamentally, is someone who is not afraid of space. The coward lives in constant terror of space. When the coward is alone in the forest and doesn't hear a sound, he thinks there is a ghost lurking somewhere. In the silence he begins to bring up all kinds of monsters and demons in his mind. The coward is afraid of darkness because he can't see anything. He is afraid of silence because he can't hear anything. Cowardice is turning the unconditional into a situation of fear by inventing reference points, or conditions, of all kinds. But for the warrior, unconditionality does not have to be conditioned or limited. It does not have to be qualified as either positive or negative, but it can just be neutral—as it is.

127

The setting-sun world is afraid of space, afraid of the truth of non-reference point. In that world, people are afraid to be vulnerable. They are afraid to expose their flesh, bone, and marrow to the world outside. They are afraid to transcend the conditions or reference points they have set up for themselves. In the setting-sun world, people believe, absolutely, in their reference points. They think that, if they open themselves, they will be exposing an open wound to germs and disease. A hungry vampire may be nearby and smell the blood and come to eat them up. The setting-sun world teaches that you should guard your flesh and blood, that you should wear a suit of armor to protect yourself. But what are you really protecting yourself from? *Space*.

If you succeed in encasing yourself completely, you may feel secure but you will also feel terribly lonely. This is not the loneliness of the warrior but the loneliness of the coward—the loneliness of being trapped in the cocoon, cut off from basic human affection. You don't know how to take off your suit of armor. You have no idea how to conduct yourself without the reference point of your own security. The challenge of warriorship is to step out of the cocoon, to step out into space, by being brave and at the same time gentle. You can expose your wounds and flesh, your sore points.

Usually when you have a wound, you put a band-aid on until it heals. Then you take off the bandage and expose the healed flesh to the world outside. In this case, you expose an open wound, open flesh, unconditionally. You can be completely raw and exposed with your husband or your wife, your banker, your landlord, anyone you meet.

Out of that comes an extraordinary birth: the birth of the universal monarch. The Shambhala definition of a monarch is someone who is very raw and sensitive, willing to open his or her heart to others. That is how you become a king or queen, the ruler of your world. The way to rule the universe is to expose your heart, so that others can see your heart beating, see your red flesh, and see the blood pulsating through your veins and arteries.

Ordinarily, we think of a king in the negative sense, as someone who holds himself apart from others, hiding in his palace and creating a kingdom to shield himself from the world. Here we are speaking of opening yourself to other human beings in order to promote human welfare. The monarch's power, in the Shambhala world, comes from being very soft. It comes from opening your heart so that you share your heart with others. You have nothing to hide, no suit of armor. Your experience is naked and direct. It is even beyond naked—it is raw, uncooked.

This is the fruition of warriorship: the complete primordial realization of basic goodness. At that level, there is absolutely no doubt about basic goodness or, therefore, about yourself. When you expose your naked flesh to the universe can you say: "Should I put a second skin on? Am I too naked?" You can't. At that point, there is no room for second thoughts. You have nothing to lose and nothing to gain. You simply expose your heart completely.

130

TWENTY
AUTHENTIC PRESENCE

At this stage, the warrior's journey is based on resting in the state of warriorship, rather than struggling to take the next step. The warrior experiences a sense of relaxing in his achievement, which is not based on ego-centered concerns but on resting in unconditional confidence, free from aggression. So the journey becomes like a flower unfolding—it is a natural process of expansion.

ACHIEVING THE REALIZATION of the universal monarch, which we discussed in the last chapter, is the fruition of developing what is called the warrior's "authentic presence." In Tibetan, "authentic presence" is *wangthang*, which literally means a "field of power." However, since this term refers to a human quality, we have loosely translated it here as "authentic presence." The basic idea of authentic presence is that, because you achieve some merit or virtue, therefore that virtue begins to be reflected in your being, your presence. So authentic presence is based on cause and effect. The cause of authentic presence is the merit you accumulate, and the effect is the authentic presence itself.

There is an outer or ordinary sense of authentic presence that anyone can experience. If a person is modest and decent and exertive, then he will begin to manifest some sense of good and wholesome being to those around him. The inner meaning of authentic presence, however, is connected more specifically to the path of Shambhala warriorship. Inner authentic presence comes, not just from being a decent, good person in the ordinary sense, but it is connected to the realization of primordial space, or egolessness. The cause or the virtue that brings inner authentic presence is emptying out and letting go. You have to be without clinging. Inner authentic presence comes from exchanging yourself with others, from being able to regard other people as yourself, generously and without fixation. So the inner merit that brings inner authentic presence is the experience of nonfixed mind, mind without fixation.

When you meet a person who has inner authentic presence, you find he has an overwhelming genuineness, which might be somewhat frightening because it is so true and honest and real. You experience a sense of command radiating from the person of inner authentic presence. Although that person might be a garbage collector or a taxi driver, still he or she has an uplifted quality, which magnetizes you and commands your attention. This is not just charisma. The person with inner authentic presence has worked on himself and made a thorough and proper journey. He has earned authentic presence by letting go, and by giving up personal comfort and fixed mind.

On the one hand, authentic presence is the result of a gradual, developmental process of letting go of ego fixation. On the other hand, it is also the result of an instantaneous, magical process of letting go of fixed mind. The two always work together. The abrupt and spontaneous process that brings authentic presence is raising windhorse, or lungta, which is basically rousing the energy of basic goodness into a wind of delight and power. Although it is beyond the scope of this book to provide actual instruction in the practice of raising windhorse, I hope that you have begun to understand the basic energy of windhorse from our discussion of it. Raising windhorse is a way to cast out depression and doubt on the spot. It is not a form of exorcism but a cheering-up process. That is to say, raising windhorse invokes and actualizes the living aspect of fearlessness and bravery. It is a magical practice for transcending doubt and hesitation in order to invoke tremendous wakefulness in your state of mind. And when you have raised lungta, authentic presence occurs.

At that point, however, your experience of authentic presence may be only a glimpse. In order to sustain that glimpse and manifest that presence fully, there is a need for discipline. So there is a developmental process for deepening and furthering authentic presence. This process is called the warrior's path of the *four dignities*. This path is connected with how to incorporate more and more space into your world, so that ultimately you can achieve the realization of the universal monarch. As your world becomes more and more vast, obviously, any notion of self-centered, egotistical existence becomes increasingly remote. So the path of the four dignities is also connected with realizing egolessness. The four dignities are *meek, perky, outrageous*, and *inscrutable*. All human beings experience the four dignities in some form. Meekness is basically experiencing a humble and gentle state of being, while perkiness is connected with uplifted and youthful energy. Outrageousness is being daring and entering into situations without hope and fear, and inscrutability is the experience of fulfillment and uncontrived, spontaneous achievement.

Although everyone has some experience of these expressions of energy, unless there is actual discipline and awareness applied, there is no fundamental sense of going forward in your life, and the four dignities are buried as part of your habitual pattern rather than becoming a path towards egolessness. So fundamentally, the four dignities must be connected to the path of warriorship. In fact, they are an advanced stage on that path. The warrior is able to realize the four dignities only after he or she has developed an unshakeable conviction in basic goodness and has seen the Great Eastern Sun reflected in the experience of sacred world. At that point, the warrior is plugged into a source of energy that never runs down, the energy of windhorse, which makes the journey very powerful. So windhorse is the fuel that energizes the four dignities and authentic presence is the vehicle.

This is somewhat paradoxical: on the one hand, the four dignities are a process of developing authentic presence; on the other hand, the experience of authentic presence is what allows the path of the four dignities to unfold. To explain that somewhat, we could say simply that egolessness is both the

ground and the fruition of this journey. Unless we have some sense of letting go of ourselves, we cannot make this journey of warriorship at all. On the other hand, once we have let go, then we find that we can incorporate greater vision and greater mind. So egolessness is the thread of vastness—if such a thing can be said to exist—that runs through the entire journey. At this stage, the warrior's journey is based on resting in the state of warriorship, rather than struggling to take the next step. The warrior experiences a sense of relaxing in his achievement, which is not based on ego-centered concerns but on resting in unconditional confidence, free from aggression. So the journey becomes like a flower unfolding—it is a natural process of expansion.

The Warrior of Meek

Meekness is the first dignity. Meek here does not mean being feeble; it just means resting in a state of simplicity, being uncomplicated and, at the same time, approachable. Whether others are hostile or friendly, the warrior of meek extends a sense of kindness to himself and mercy to others. Altogether, your mind is not filled with ordinary preoccupations and you are never seduced by trivial situations. This is because your awareness allows you to refrain from activities that dim the vision of the Great Eastern Sun. Therefore, you always remain meek and well-disciplined.

The principle of meekness has three stages. The first is that, because the warrior is modest, his mind is never bloated by poisonous arrogance. Modesty does not mean thinking of yourself as tiny or small. Modesty here means feeling true and genuine. Therefore the warrior feels self-contained, with no need for external reference points to confirm him. Part of modesty is an underlying brilliance, being self-contained but shining out. The warrior's awareness shines out with tremendous inquisitiveness, a keen interest in everything around him. You begin to see things as natural messages, rather than as reference points for your existence. The difference between ordinary inquisitiveness and that of the warrior's path of meek is that the warrior's awareness is always joined with discipline. Therefore you don't miss anything; you see every detail. Such disciplined awareness is clearing the ground in such a way that the universe begins to become part of your vision.

The second stage of meekness is the expression of unconditional confidence. The analogy for meekness is a tiger in its prime, who moves slowly but heedfully through the jungle. In this case, the tiger is not searching for prey. He is not stalking in the jungle, hoping to pounce on other animals. Rather, the image of the tiger expresses a combination of self-satisfaction and modesty. The tiger walks slowly through the jungle, with mindfulness. But because the tiger likes his body and his bounciness and sense of rhythm, he is relaxed. From the tip of his nose to the tip of his tail, there are no problems. His movements are like waves; he swims through the jungle. So his watchfulness is accompanied by relaxation and confidence. This is the analogy for the warrior's confidence. For the warrior of meek, confidence is a natural state of awareness and mindfulness in the way he conducts his affairs.

The third stage of meek is that, because there is no hesitation, the warrior's mind is vast. His mind is uplifted and sees beyond the limits of the sky. Vastness here does not come from seeing a great future in front of you, expecting that you are going to be perky and outrageous and inscrutable and finally realize the greatest warriorship of all. Rather, vastness comes from seeing the greatness of your own spot, your own particular place. You realize that your basic state of mind is no longer an issue, nor is your relationship to Shambhala vision and the Great Eastern Sun. So both ambition and a poverty-stricken mentality are overcome. Vast mind also comes from sharing the vision of the dralas. You actually are able to jump into that vast and powerful ocean of magic, which may be painful or pleasurable, but nevertheless delightful.

The fruition of meekness is that, because the warrior possesses extraordinary exertion, he is able to accomplish whatever purposes or objectives he is trying to fulfill. The sense of exertion is not speedy, aggressive, or heavy-handed. Like the tiger in the jungle, you are both relaxed and energized. You are constantly inquisitive but your awareness is also disciplined, so you accomplish every activity without difficulty, and you inspire those around you to do the same.

The warrior of meek has abandoned gain, victory, and fame, leaving them far behind. You are not dependent on feedback from others, because you have no doubt about yourself. You do not rely on encouragement or discouragement; therefore, you also have no need to display your valor to others. Self-respect is a very rare occurrence in the ordinary setting-sun world. But when you raise your windhorse, you feel good and trust yourself. Therefore, because you respect yourself, you do not have to depend on gain and victory. And because you trust yourself, it is unnecessary to be fearful of others. So the warrior of meek does not need to deviously trick others; therefore, his dignity is never diminished.

So meekness provides vast vision and confidence. The four dignities begin from this humble and dutiful but vast vision, which at the same time sees the details with a sense of meticulousness. The beginning of the journey is this natural sense of fulfillment that doesn't need to beg from others.

The Warrior of Perky

The principle of perky is symbolized by a snow lion who enjoys the freshness of the highland mountains. The snow lion is vibrant, energetic, and also youthful. He roams the highlands where the atmosphere is clear and the air is fresh. The surroundings are wild flowers, a few trees, and occasional boulders and rocks. The atmosphere is fresh and new and also has a sense of goodness and cheerfulness. Perky does not mean that one is perked up by temporary situations, but it refers to unconditional cheerfulness, which comes from ongoing discipline. Just as the snow lion enjoys the refreshing air, the warrior of perky is constantly disciplined and continuously enjoys discipline. For him, discipline is not a demand but a pleasure.

There are two stages of perkiness. The first one is experiencing an uplifted and joyful mind. In this case, uplifted mind means a continual state of delight that is not caused by anything. At the same time, this experience of joyful mind comes from the meekness you have previously experienced. So we could say that perkiness is due to meekness. The modesty, mindfulness, and brilliance of meek bring a natural sense of delight. From that joyful mind, the warrior of perky develops artfulness in whatever actions he performs. His action is always beautiful and dignified.

The second stage of perky is that the warrior of perky is never caught in the trap of doubt. The fundamental doubt is doubting yourself, which, as we discussed in Chapter Five, occurs when body and mind are unsynchronized. This doubt can manifest as anxiety or jealousy or arrogance, or, in its extreme form, as slandering others because you doubt your own confidence. The warrior of perky rests in the state of trust that comes from meekness. Therefore he has no doubt, and because of that, he never enters what are known as the lower realms. The lower realms refer to living purely for the sake of survival. There are different aspects of the lower realms. One is living purely out of animal instinct, as though your whole survival were based on killing others and eating them up. The second aspect is that you are stricken with a poverty mentality. You experience constant hunger and fear of losing your life. The third possibility is experiencing a constant state of turmoil and living in a world of paranoia, where you torment yourself. Because the warrior of perky is free from doubt and practices continuous discipline, he is free from the lower realms. Free from these, the warrior of perky possesses all the goodness of the higher realms. Being in the higher realms refers to being clear and precise. This warrior is always aware and never confused as to what to accept and what to reject.

In summary, because of the meekness and gentleness that have occurred in the previous stage of warriorship, you make a further journey into perkiness. The warrior of perky is never caught in the trap of doubt and is always joyful and artful. Because you are never enslaved in the lower realms, there is no confusion and dullness. This brings the attainment of a wholesome life. So the fruition, or the ultimate notion, of perky is that you achieve a wholesome body and mind and the synchronization of the two. The warrior of perky is both humble and uplifted, as well as fundamentally youthful.

The Warrior of Outrageous

Outrageousness does not mean being unreasonable or, for that matter, wild. Outrageousness here refers to possessing the strength and power of warriorship. Outrageousness is based on the achievement of fearlessness, which means going completely beyond fear. In order to overcome fear, it is also necessary to overcome hope. When you hope for something in your life, if it doesn't happen, you are disappointed or upset. If it does happen, then you become elated and excited. You are constantly riding a roller coaster up and down. Because he has never encountered any doubt about himself at all, therefore the warrior of outrageous has nothing to hope for and nothing to fear. So it is said that the warrior of outrageous is never caught in the ambush of hope, and therefore fearlessness is achieved.

Outrageousness is symbolized by the garuda, a legendary Tibetan bird who is traditionally referred to as the king of birds. The garuda hatches full-grown from its egg and soars into outer space, expanding and stretching its wings, beyond any limits. Likewise, having overcome hope and fear, the warrior of outrageous develops a sense of great freedom. So the state of mind of outrageousness is very vast. Your mind fathoms the whole of space. You go beyond any possibilities of holding back at all. You just go and go and go, completely expanding yourself. And like the garuda king, the warrior of outrageous finds nothing to obstruct his vast mind.

Because there is no obstruction, the warrior of outrageous has no intention of measuring the space. You have no anxiety about how far you can go or how much you should contain yourself. You have completely abandoned those reference points for measuring your progress. So you experience tremendous relaxation. Outrageousness is that vast mind which has gone beyond the beyond. The analogy for this is a good, self-existing sword—desire to sharpen it will make it dull. If you try to apply a competitive or comparative logic to the experience of vast mind, by trying to measure how much space you have fathomed, how much is left to fathom, or how much someone else has fathomed, you are just dulling your sword. It is futile and counterproductive. In contrast to that approach, outrageousness is accomplishment without a sense of accomplisher, without reference point.

In short, because he is free from hope and fear, the warrior of outrageous soars in outer space, like the garuda king. In this space, you see no fear and no imperfection. Therefore you experience a greater world and attain greater mind. Such attainment is, of course, based on the warrior's training of meek and perky. Because of these, you can be outrageous. The warrior of outrageous also possesses great mercy for others. Because you have no obstacles to expanding your vision, you have immense capabilities of working for others. You are able to help them, providing whatever is needed.

The Warrior of Inscrutable

Inscrutability is represented by the dragon. The dragon is energetic, powerful, and unwavering. But these qualities of the dragon do not stand alone without the meekness of the tiger, the perkiness of the lion, and the outrageousness of the garuda.

Inscrutability falls into two categories. First there is the state of inscrutability, and second the expression of inscrutability. The state of inscrutability is based on fearlessness. This is unlike the conventional concept of inscrutability, which is deviousness or a blank wall. For the warrior of inscrutable, fearlessness has been achieved, particularly from the previous experience of outrageousness. From that fearlessness, you develop gentleness and sympathy, which allow you to be noncommittal, but with a sense of humor. In this case we are talking about a state of being, just like the state of being of the dragon who enjoys resting in the sky among the clouds and the wind. However, that state is not static. Just as a solid oak tree is swayed by the wind, so a sense of humor makes a person playful. Because of this playfulness and humor, there is no room for depression. The state of inscrutability is therefore joyous and methodical.

According to tradition, the dragon abides in the sky in the summer, and hibernates in the ground during the winter. When the spring comes, the dragon rises from the ground with the mist and the dew. When a storm is necessary, the dragon breathes out lightning and roars out thunder. This analogy gives us some feeling of predictability within the context of unpredictability. Inscrutability is also the state of settling down in your confidence—remaining solid and relaxed at once. You are open and fearless, free from longing and doubt, but at the same time, you are very interested in the movements of the world. Your wakefulness and intelligence make you self-contained and confident with a confidence that needs no reaffirmation through feedback. So the

140

state of inscrutability is conviction that doesn't need confirmation. You feel a sense of genuineness, that you are not deceiving yourself or others. That notion comes from being settled.

Inscrutability is a state of wholesomeness within which there is no gap or hesitation. It is therefore a sense of truly living, of actually leading your life; it is a feeling of hardcore solidity, but at the same time you are continuously sharpening your intelligence. Question and answer occur simultaneously and therefore inscrutability is continuous. It is also unyielding; it never gives in; you do not change your mind. If the course of a procedure is threatened, the mind of inscrutability responds with deadly accuracy, not because of aggression but because of its basic confidence.

The expression of inscrutability is how inscrutability manifests itself in action. The main point is being somewhat noncommittal, but at the same time seeing a project through to its end. You are noncommittal because you are not interested in confirmation. This does not mean that you are afraid of being caught by your actions, but rather that you are not interested in being at the center of the scene. However, at the same time, you are very loyal to others, so that you always accomplish your project with sympathy for them.

The manifestation of inscrutability is methodical and elegant. The way of exercising inscrutability is that you don't spell out the truth. You imply the truth, with wakeful delight in your accomplishment. What is wrong with spelling out the truth? When you spell out the truth it loses its essence and becomes either "my" truth or "your" truth; it becomes an end in itself. When you spell out the truth you are spending your capital while no one gets any profit. It becomes undignified, a giveaway. By implying the truth, the truth doesn't become anyone's property. When the dragon wants a rainstorm he causes thunder and lightning. That brings the rain. Truth is generated from its environment; in that way it becomes a powerful reality. From this point of view, studying the imprint of the truth is more important than the truth itself. The truth doesn't need a handle.

The vision of inscrutability is to create an orderly and powerful world full of gentle energy. So the warrior of inscrutable is not in a rush. You begin at the beginning. First you look for the ignition. Then, cultivating that beginning, you find a sympathetic environment in which to start the action. By not jumping to conclusions, you discover both positive and negative conditions. Then you find further starting points. By not holding on to what you have, but by generating more sympathetic environments, you playfully proceed to the next step. That provides refreshment; you are not suffocated by the course of action you are taking. The warrior never becomes a slave of his own deed.

So the action of inscrutability is to create an environment which contains fearlessness, warmth, and genuineness. If there is no appreciation of or interest in the world, it is difficult to accomplish inscrutability. Fearfulness and cowardice bring depression. Not having a sense of delight brings no room to be inscrutable.

Authentic presence brings meekness, perkiness, outrageousness, and ultimately achieves inscrutability. Naturally the apprentice warrior must go through training, starting with the right attitude to life, which is not necessarily seeing the world as an amusement park, but nonetheless experiencing delight and leading your life elegantly. Pain and depression, as well as pleasure, may be source materials for study. A sense of wholesomeness makes life worth living; a sense of genuineness brings confidence.

The experience of inscrutability is not a calculating one. It is not learning a new trick nor is it mimicking someone else. When you are at ease, you find a state of true healthy mind. The cultivation of inscrutability is to learn to be. It has been said that everyone possesses the potentiality to be confident. When we speak of confidence here we refer to enlightened confidence—not to confidence in something, but just to being *confident*. This confidence is unconditional. Inscrutability is a spark that is free from any analytical scheme. When meeting a situation, challenge and interest occur simultaneously. You proceed with an open mind and with direct action. This brings delight, and guidelines evolve naturally.

Inscrutability comes from giving rather than taking. As you give, you find services available automatically—thus the warrior conquers the world. Such a notion of generosity brings freedom from inhibition. Then relaxation develops.

The warrior doesn't have to struggle. A sense of struggle is not the style of inscrutability. The apprentice might feel impatient or inadequate. At that point you have to be inscrutable to yourself. Slowing down any impulse is said to be the best way to begin. When the warrior feels a sense of leadership and order on earth, that appreciation brings some kind of breakthrough. The closed and poverty-stricken world begins to fall apart, and from that feeling of freedom, you begin to appreciate natural hierarchy; you are a part of it. Then inscrutability becomes the natural way, including respect for elders, sympathy for kin, and confidence in colleagues. At that point learning is no struggle, and blockages are overcome.

When we talk of hierarchy, we refer to the structure and order of the universe—a sense of heritage that the warrior must appreciate. But appreciating it is not enough. There is a need for discipline, and that discipline comes from realizing that such a world as this was created for you, that people expended energy to bring you up, that in your weak moments you were helped, and that, when you were ready for inspiration, you were inspired. So the discipline of genuinely working for others comes from appreciating hierarchy.

Inscrutability is brilliant and fearless because the warrior is guided by the vision of the Great Eastern Sun. With exertion and delight you can lift yourself up, in order to achieve authentic presence and, ultimately, the state of being of the universal monarch. By opening yourself and fearlessly giving to others, you can help to create a powerful world of warriors.

TWENTY-ONE

THE SHAMBHALA LINEAGE

*The idea of lineage in the Shambhala teachings re-
lates to one's connection with primordial wisdom.
That wisdom is accessible and extremely simple,
but also vast and profound.*

MAKING THE JOURNEY OF WARRIORSHIP depends first of all on
your personal realization of genuineness and basic goodness.
However, in order to continue the journey, in order to tread
the path of the four dignities and achieve authentic presence,
it is necessary to have a guide—a master warrior to show you
the way. Ultimately, giving up selfishness, or ego, is only
possible if you have a living, human example—someone who
has already done so, and therefore makes it possible for you
to do the same.

In this chapter, we are going to discuss the notion of
lineage in the Shambhala teachings, that is, how the complete realization of sanity can be handed down to a human
being in the Shambhala world so that he or she can embody
that sanity and promote its attainment in others. So in this
chapter we are going to consider the qualities of the master
warrior and how they are transmitted, both to him and by
him.

Fundamentally, the notion of lineage in the Shambhala

teachings is connected with how the wisdom of the cosmic mirror, which we discussed in Part Two, is transmitted and continued in human life, human existence. To review briefly, the quality of the cosmic mirror is that it is unconditioned, vast open space. It is an eternal and completely open space, space beyond question. In the realm of the cosmic mirror, your mind extends its vision completely, beyond doubt. Before thoughts, before the thinking process takes place, there is the accommodation of the cosmic mirror, which has no boundary—no center and no fringe. As we discussed, the way to experience this space is through the sitting practice of meditation.

As we discussed in Chapter Twelve, "Discovering Magic," experiencing the realm of the cosmic mirror gives rise to wisdom—the wisdom of vast and deep perception, beyond conflict, which is called *drala*. There are various levels of experiencing drala. The primordial or ultimate level of drala is experiencing directly the wisdom of the cosmic mirror. When you experience that wisdom, then you are contacting the origin of the Shambhala lineage, the source of wisdom.

In the first chapter of this book we discussed the myths surrounding the historical kingdom of Shambhala and the Shambhala rulers. As we discussed there, some people believe that this kingdom still lies hidden somewhere on earth, while others see the kingdom as a metaphor or even believe that it ascended to the heavens at some point. But according to the way in which we have been discussing the Shambhala teachings, the source of these teachings, or we could say, the kingdom of Shambhala itself, is not some mysterious heavenly realm. It is the realm of the cosmic mirror, the primordial realm that is always available to human beings if they relax and expand their minds. From this point of view, the imperial rulers of Shambhala, who are called the Rigden kings, are the inhabitants of the cosmic mirror. They are the primordial manifestation of the wisdom of vast mind, the ultimate wisdom of drala. Therefore, they are referred to as ultimate drala.

Ultimate drala has three characteristics. First, it is primordial, which as we have discussed, is not going back to the Stone Age or something prehistoric, but it is going one step beyond or before we ever think of anything at all. That is the state of being of the Rigden kings who occupy the cosmic mirror as their kingdom. The second quality is unchanging-ness. There are no second thoughts in the realm of the Rigden kings. Second thought refers to flickering mind, not having confidence in the purity of your perception, so that your mind wavers and hesitates. Here there are no second thoughts. It is an unchanging realm, completely unchanging. The third quality of ultimate drala is bravery. Bravery means you are not giving in even to any potential doubts; in fact, there is no room for any doubts whatsoever in this realm.

So, when you contact the wisdom of the cosmic mirror, you are meeting the ultimate dralas, the Rigden kings of Shambhala. Their vast vision lies behind all the activities of mankind, in the open, unconditioned space of mind itself. In that way, they watch over and protect human affairs, so to speak. However, this is quite different from the notion that the Rigdens are living on some celestial plane, from which they look down at the earth.

Once having made a connection to ultimate drala, it is possible for the primordial wisdom and vision of the Rigden kings to be passed down to the level of human perception. As we discussed in "Discovering Magic," the vastness of percep-tion can be captured in simplicity, a single perception, on the spot. When we allow vastness to enter our perception, then it becomes drala; it becomes brilliant and luminous—magical. When we have this experience, then we are meeting what are called the inner dralas. The inner dralas are empowered by the wisdom of the cosmic mirror, the Rigdens, to manifest brilliance and elegance in this phenomenal world. The inner dralas are divided into the mother and father lineages. The mother lineage represents gentleness and the father lineage represents fearlessness. Gentleness and fearlessness are the first two qualities of inner drala. When someone is actually able to dwell in the world of brilliance and freedom from accepting and rejecting, the world of experiencing drala in all phenomena, then he or she automatically experiences tre-mendous gentleness and fearlessness in that space.

The third quality of inner drala is intelligence, or discriminating awareness, which binds together gentleness and fearlessness. With discriminating awareness, gentleness is not ordinary gentleness, but it becomes the experience of sacred world. And fearlessness goes beyond bravado to manifest elegance and richness in a person's life. So the basic sharpness of awareness binds gentleness and fearlessness to create the warrior's world of vast but appreciative perception.

Finally, the wisdom of ultimate and inner drala can be transmitted to a living human being. In other words, by realizing completely the cosmic mirror principle of unconditionality and by invoking that principle utterly in the brilliant perception of reality, a human being can become living drala—living magic. That is how one joins the lineage of Shambhala warriors and becomes a master warrior—not just by invoking but by *embodying* drala. So the master warrior embodies the outer drala principle.

The basic quality of the master warrior is that his presence evokes the experience of the cosmic mirror and the magic of perception in others. That is, his very being transcends duality on the spot, and thus he is said to have complete authentic presence. When the warrior students experience this overwhelming genuineness, it allows them and provokes them to go beyond their own selfishness, beyond ego, in an instant.

This, I think, is a rather difficult concept to grasp, so perhaps we should talk in greater depth about the qualities of the master warrior, so that this becomes more clear. To begin with, the birth of the master warrior takes place in the realm of the cosmic mirror, where there is no beginning or end—there is simply a state of vastness. His realization, or his state of being, is not purely the result of training or philosophy. Rather he has relaxed completely into the unconditional purity of the cosmic mirror. Therefore, he has experienced unconditional wakefulness, free from ego. Because he always has access to that unconditioned space, he is never subject to the confusion or sleepiness of selfishness, at all. He is totally awake. And thus, also, the energy of the master warrior is always connected with ultimate drala, the vast vision of the Rigden kings. So he is free from confusion.

Secondly, because the master warrior has completely identified himself with the lineage of wisdom of the Rigden kings, he begins to develop great tenderness, great compassion, which is witnessing basic goodness in all beings. When the master warrior views the world around him, he *knows* that all human beings possess basic goodness and that they are entitled to realize the principle of their own genuineness, at least. And beyond that, they have the possibility to give birth to the universal monarch in themselves. Therefore, great generosity and great compassion take place in the mind of the master warrior.

He finds that the Great Eastern Sun has entered his heart completely, so completely that he actually manifests the brilliance of the Great Eastern Sun, extending its light rays to sentient beings who suffer in the twilight of the setting sun. The master warrior sees the complete path of warriorship, and he is able to extend that path, provide that path, to warrior students—to any human being who longs to fulfill his or her precious human birth.

Finally, the master warrior, out of his great compassion for human beings, is able to join heaven and earth. That is to say, the ideals of human beings and the ground where human beings stand can be joined together by the power of the master warrior. Then heaven and earth begin to dance with each other, and human beings feel that there is no quarrel about who possesses the best part of heaven or the worst part of earth.

In order to join heaven and earth, you need confidence and trust in yourself. But then beyond that, in joining heaven and earth, you have to go beyond selfishness. You have to be without selfishness. If someone thinks: "Now I have it? Ha, ha!"—that doesn't work. Joining heaven and earth happens only if you go beyond an egoistic attitude. No one can join heaven and earth together if he is selfish, because then he has neither heaven nor earth. He is stuck instead in a plastic realm, an artificial realm, which is horrific. Joining heaven and earth comes only from being beyond desire—beyond your selfish needs. It comes from passionlessness, transcending desire. If the master warrior were drunk on his own authentic presence, then it would be disastrous. Therefore, the master warrior is very humble, extremely humble. His humbleness comes from working with others. When you work with others, you realize the need to be patient, to give space and time to others to develop their own understanding of goodness and of warriorship. If you are frantic and try to push basic goodness onto others, then nothing happens except further chaos. Knowing that, you become extremely humble and patient in working with others. You let things assume their own shape in their own time. So patience is extending gentleness and faith to others all the time. You never lose faith in their basic goodness, in their ability to actualize nowness and sacredness, in their ability to become warriors in the world.

The master warrior guides his students with patience, and he also provides gentleness—being without aggression. Then, he also guides his students by being true—being stable and solid. If truth were like a fluttering flag in the wind, you would never know which side you were looking at. So the idea here is that being true is being solid and completely stable, like a mountain. You can rely on the sanity of the master warrior; it never wavers. He is completely genuine.

Because there is no fear in the master warrior's own state of mind or in his physical being, the process of helping others takes place constantly. The mind of the master warrior is thoroughly free from laziness. In extending himself fearlessly to others, the master warrior expresses intense interest in the activities of his students—from the level of what they have for dinner up to the level of their state of mind, whether they are happy or sad, joyful or depressed. So mutual humor and appreciation can take place naturally between the master warrior and the warrior students.

But most important, in every activity of his life, in every action he takes, there is always magic—always. In whatever he does, the master warrior of Shambhala guides the minds of his students into the visionary mind of the Rigden kings, the space of the cosmic mirror. He constantly challenges his students to step beyond themselves, to step out into the vast and brilliant world of reality in which he abides. The challenge that he provides is not so much that he is always setting hurdles for his students or egging them on. Rather, his authentic presence is a constant challenge to be genuine and true.

Altogether then, the idea of lineage in the Shambhala

teachings relates to one's connection with primordial wisdom. That wisdom is accessible and extremely simple, but also vast and profound. The way to despotism and corruption lies in clinging to concepts, without access to a pure realm in which hope and fear are unknown. In the realm of the cosmic mirror, clinging to concept and doubt has never been heard of, and those who have proclaimed the true goodness, the innate primordial goodness, of human beings, have always had access to this realm, in some form.

Over the centuries, there have been many who have sought the ultimate good and have tried to share it with their fellow human beings. To realize it requires immaculate discipline and unflinching conviction. Those who have been fearless in their search and fearless in their proclamation belong to the lineage of master warriors, whatever their religion, philosophy, or creed. What distinguishes such leaders of humanity and guardians of human wisdom is their fearless expression of gentleness and genuineness—on behalf of all sentient beings. We should venerate their example and acknowledge the path that they have laid for us. They are the fathers and mothers of Shambhala, who make it possible, in the midst of this degraded age, to contemplate enlightened society.

APPENDIX

THE SHAMBHALA TRAINING PROGRAM

The sitting practice of meditation is the foundation for the realization and understanding of all of the principles discussed in this book. For those interested in pursuing the path of warriorship outlined here, Shambhala Training presents a series of weekend programs that introduce the sitting practice of meditation, as well as the principles of Shambhala vision. The first night of the program is a free introductory lecture. During the weekend, personal instruction in meditation and individual meetings with a program director are provided, as well as lectures, discussion groups, and extended periods of meditation practice.

Shambhala Training is divided into five levels of study:
Level I   Ordinary Magic
Level II   The Birth of a Warrior
Level III Warrior in the World
Level IV Awakened Heart
Level V   Open Sky: Primordial Stroke

Shambhala Training also offers a graduate program of study for those who complete Level V and sponsors various cultural and social events, open to participants, friends, and interested public.

As of this printing, Shambhala Training centers have been established in the following cities in the United States, Canada, and Europe:

UNITED STATES
Atlanta, Georgia
Austin, Texas
Baltimore, Maryland
Berkeley, California
Boston, Massachusetts
Boulder, Colorado
Burlington, Vermont
Chicago, Illinois
Los Angeles, California
New York, New York
Northampton, Massachusetts
Palo Alto, California
Philadelphia, Pennsylvania
San Francisco, California
Seattle, Washington
Washington, D. C.

CANADA
Halifax, Nova Scotia
Montreal, Quebec
Ottawa, Ontario
Toronto, Ontario
Vancouver, British Columbia

EUROPE
London, England
Marburg, West Germany

For information on the Shambhala Training center nearest to you, please contact:

Shambhala Training
2130 Arapahoe
Boulder, Colorado 80302
Phone: 303-444-7881

INDEX

INDEX

natural hierarchy *(continued)*
  heaven, earth, and man
  (principles), 100–102; and
  lha, nyen, and *lu,* 105–111
"no," learning to say, 49
nonaggression, 10, 91; as
  satyagraha (Skt. "seizing
  the truth"), 116
nonexistent heart, 23
non-reference point, 126–128;
  discovery of, 126; truth of,
  126. *See also* basic goodness,
  unconditional; egolessness
nowness, 67–73, 74–75, 88; of
  cosmic mirror, 75, 76; and
  enlightened society, 72; lack
  of, and corruption, 72–73
Now We Are Six, 78
nyen (principle), 106. See also
  lha, nyen, and *lu*

obstacle(s), to invoking
  drala, 89, 91, 93, 97
others: exchanging yourself with,
  132; working for, 68,
  139–140, 143. *See also*
  helping others
outer drala(s), 147–149; as master
  warrior, 147–149
outrageousness, 133, 138–140;
  vast mind of, 139

patience, of master warrior, 149
pawo. See warrior
perception: depth of, 79; as drala,
  77–80, 146; as magic, 77–
  80, 146; supernatural, 77; and
  the vision of the Rigden
  kings, 146; warrior's world of,
  147; wisdom of, 76, 145
perception(s), 76–80, 147; act of,
  76; fields (objects) of, 76;
  organs of, 76. *See also* sense
  perceptions
perkiness, 133, 137–138; fruition
  of, 138; two stages of, 137–
  138

politics and poverty, 115–116
polyester leisure suits, 85
posture, 16–17, 51–52; meditation, 16–17, 18; universal, 17
power, field of. *See* authentic
  presence
primordial mirror. *See* cosmic
  mirror
protocol: purpose of, 90; ultimate,
  108

queen, 117, 118, 128. *See also*
  seven riches of the
  universal monarch

reality, 10–12, 74–75, 113:
  domestic, 11–12, 68–69
  dralas of, 80
  of fear, 24
  magic of, 82, 83
  and nowness, 72–73, 74–75
  of setting-sun world, 34–35, 39
  unconditionality of, 76
realm, of cosmic mirror, 145–146;
  as realm of Rigden kings,
  145
realm(s):
  higher, 138
  lower, 138
  of perceptions, 76
reference point(s). *See* nonreference
  point
relaxation, 75–76; and discipline,
  55; ideal state of, 75–76;
  and inscrutability, 142–143
renunciation, 42–46, 47; definition
  of, 43; discipline of, 45–
  46, 55; and privacy, 43,
  45–46
restlessness, as form of fear,
  24
richness. *See* wealth
richness, 114–119; basic practice
  of, 116–117; seven principles of, 117–118. *See also*
  seven riches, of the
  universal monarch

160

༄། །ཁར་ཆེན་གསེར་གྱི་ཉི་མའི་གཉེན་འཇིང་ཀྱིས། །
རིགས་ལྡན་ཡེ་ཤེས་པ་དང་ཚུལ་བཞིན་པ་དང་། །
འགྲོ་བའི་མ་རིག་མུན་པ་སེལ་ནས་ཀྱང་། །
རབ་གསལ་དཔལ་ལ་འགྲོ་ཀུན་སྒྲོད་གྱུར་ཅིག །

By the confidence of the Golden Sun of the Great East
May the lotus garden of the Rigdens' wisdom bloom
May the dark ignorance of sentient beings be dispelled
May all beings enjoy profound brilliant glory

ABOUT THE AUTHOR

CHÖGYAM TRUNGPA, the founder of Shambhala Training, is also the founder and president of Naropa Institute, an innovative liberal arts college. He is, as well, the president of Vajradhatu, an association of more than one hundred Buddhist meditation and study centers in the United States, Canada, and Europe.

A lineage holder and meditation master in the Kagyü school of Tibetan Buddhism, Chögyam Trungpa was the supreme abbot of the Surmang Monasteries in Tibet, where he also received the degree of Khyenpo, roughly equivalent to a Doctor of Divinity degree in the West. As part of his education in Tibet, Chögyam Trungpa also studied and practiced traditional artistic disciplines such as calligraphy, poetry, dance, and thangka painting.

In 1959, forced to escape his homeland, the author fled to India. There, by appointment by His Holiness the Dalai Lama, he served as the spiritual advisor to the Young Lamas' Home School. In 1963 he travelled to England, where he attended Oxford University as a Spaulding Fellow. There, he studied Western philosophy, religion, art, and language. While at Oxford, Chögyam Trungpa also studied Japanese flower arrangement with Stella Coe, and he received an instructor's degree in the Sogetsu School of flower arranging.

In 1970 Chögyam Trungpa was invited to the United States. Since that time, he has made his home in Boulder, Colorado, and he has been teaching throughout the United States, Canada, and Europe. He is the author of many popular books on Buddhism and the path of meditation, among them *Meditation in Action, Cutting Through Spiritual Materialism, The Myth of Freedom,* and *Journey without Goal*. This is his first book on the Shambhala teachings.

Widely known as a meditation master, teacher, and scholar, Chögyam Trungpa is also an artist who has exhibited his calligraphies, flower arrangements, and environmental designs in galleries in San Francisco, Los Angeles, and the Denver-Boulder area. A film on his artistic work, "Discovering Elegance," is available through Centre Productions in Boulder, Colorado.

For information on Shambhala Training, please see the Appendix. For information on programs offered by Naropa Institute, please write to the Institute at 2130 Arapahoe, Boulder, Colorado 80302. Information on any of the Vajradhatu centers may be obtained by writing to Vajradhatu at 1345 Spruce Street, Boulder, Colorado 80302.